THE UNOFFICIAL SIMPSONS COOKBOOK

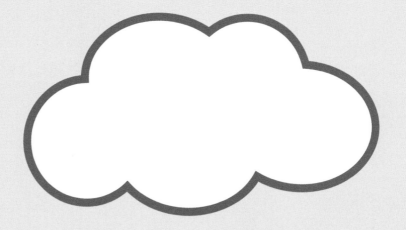

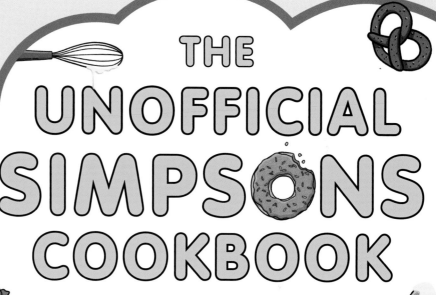

THE UNOFFICIAL SIMPSONS COOKBOOK

From Krusty Burgers to
Marge's Pretzels, Famous Recipes from
Your Favorite Cartoon Family

LAUREL RANDOLPH

Foreword by Bill Oakley, Former Showrunner of *The Simpsons*

Adams Media

New York London Toronto Sydney New Delhi

Adams Media
An Imprint of Simon & Schuster, Inc.
100 Technology Center Drive
Stoughton, Massachusetts 02072

First Adams Media hardcover edition August 2021

ADAMS MEDIA and colophon are trademarks of Simon & Schuster.

For information about special discounts for bulk purchases, please contact Simon & Schuster Special Sales at 1-866-506-1949 or business@simonandschuster.com.

The Simon & Schuster Speakers Bureau can bring authors to your live event. For more information or to book an event contact the Simon & Schuster Speakers Bureau at 1-866-248-3049 or visit our website at www.simonspeakers.com.

Interior design by Sylvia McArdle
Photographs by Harper Point Photography
Illustrations by Priscilla Yuen

Manufactured in the United States of America

1 2021

Library of Congress Cataloging-in-Publication Data
Names: Randolph, Laurel, author.
Title: The unofficial Simpsons cookbook / Laurel Randolph.
Description: First Adams Media hardcover edition. | Stoughton, MA: Adams Media, 2021 | Series: Unofficial cookbook | Includes index.
Identifiers: LCCN 2021003296 | ISBN 9781507215890 (hc) | ISBN 9781507215906 (ebook)
Subjects: LCSH: Simpsons (Television program) | Cooking, American. | Food on television. | LCGFT: Cookbooks.
Classification: LCC TX715 .R21458 2021 | DDC 641.5973--dc23
LC record available at https://lccn.loc.gov/2021003296

ISBN 978-1-5072-1589-0
ISBN 978-1-5072-1590-6 (ebook)

For Dan,
You came and you found me a turkey,
on my vacation away from workie.

CONTENTS

Chapter 4
DINNER 76

Chapter 5
DESSERT 99

Chapter 6
DRINKS 130

ACKNOWLEDGMENTS

Huge thanks to my team of recipe testers: Lillian, Sean, Jennifer, Mike, Jef, Bethany, Hannah, Meg, Laura, Vicki, Keri, Sam, Sara, Ryan, Melinda, Daphne, Jeremy, Joe, and Whitney. Thanks to Eat Like Kings for the doughnut advice. Thanks to my husband, Dan, for embiggening my life. Thanks to my agent, Danielle; my editor, Eileen; and Sylvia and the rest of the design team. Thanks to Bill Oakley and Julia Prescott. I just think you're neat!

FOREWORD

The world of Springfield is intentionally crummy. The town is beset with an inextinguishable tire yard fire, a slipshod nuclear power plant, a decaying elementary school, and a hundred other fifth-rate taverns, hospitals, shops, and burlesque houses (though La Maison Derrière is actually well above par).

Nonetheless, a lot of boneheads (including me) yearn to visit the world of Springfield—so much so that not one, but two amusement parks have actually constructed popular attractions based on the town. But those places are expensive, and because they are in business to make money, the food is too *good*. Universal Studios is not going to sell you an authentic Homer's Patented Space-Age Out-of-This-World Moon Waffle or Nachos, Flanders-Style, because the general food-eating public would be scratching their heads and quickly departing for the nearest Wendy's.

But you, me, us Simpsons fans—we yearn for the real stuff: Martin's Raisin Roundies, IRS-wiches, the Dryyyyyy Crackers that Kirk Van Houten devoted his career to before getting the boot without so much as a "good luck."

As a former writer and showrunner of *The Simpsons* (and now an *Instagram* food "personality"), I think it is particularly thrilling to delve into this world because, honestly, nonstop eating was such an important part of working on the show way back when—that's why there are so many food jokes! As we wrote in the early seasons, there were no cell phones to distract us from the arduous, unending script rewrites. Instead, we turned to food, obsessing endlessly over lunch orders and the contents of the snack room next door, eating the free promotional Butterfingers they sent us, and slowly gaining way too much weight (I lost 65 pounds after I left the show!).

It was a regular occurrence for a writer to order a whole pie for lunch, put it in the refrigerator, and slowly eat piece after piece throughout the afternoon for amusement. Someone (maybe it was me) got in the habit of ordering three shrimp cocktails for lunch, having one, and taking the other two home to eat for dinner. One time—to, er, test the limits of the system for abuse—I ordered caviar for dinner. News of that got around, believe me. When we were not eating, we were dreaming up new foods: TUBBB!, Uncle Jim's Country Fillin', the Strawberrito, Corn Nog, you name it.

Now many of these fictional items—the foods that built Springfield—are ours for the tasting, courtesy of the hard (and slightly demented) work of mad kitchen scientist Laurel Randolph! Best of all, she has improved the taste of many and removed the toxic or poisonous ingredients so that few, if any, may actually kill you ("not a guarantee").

From improvised freak shows like Homer's Clove and Tom Collins Pie to carefully prepared freak shows like Mr. Burns's Fig Cake to professionally cooked train wrecks like Moe's Hobo Chicken Chili, you will find within this work a staggering array of Simpsons foods that you have dreamed of trying if you are a complete weirdo. Join your fellow weirdos in a Floor Pie or Flaming Moe, if you dare!

And since the recipe for TUBBB! does not actually appear in this work, I will close by adding it here:

TUBBB!

1 (48-ounce) can vegetable shortening
9 pounds powdered sugar
3 tablespoons vanilla extract

Dump all ingredients into a 1-gallon plastic bucket and beat until blended. For best results, eat with a large spoon while watching nine consecutive hours of reality shows. Warning: This recipe might actually kill you.

Obviously grilled,
I remain,
Bill Oakley
@thatbilloakley on *Instagram*

INTRODUCTION

Mmm...cookbook. Have you ever watched Homer gobbling up a doughnut and wished you could enjoy it too? Or followed Marge whipping together meal after meal in her colorful kitchen and longed for a seat at the table? Pull up a chair!

In *The Unofficial Simpsons Cookbook* you'll find seventy perfectly cromulent recipes from your favorite cartoon, *The Simpsons*. Now you can enjoy the show's iconic dishes in the comfort of your own home, with or without the corncob curtains. Besides, what's the point of going out? You're just going to wind up back here anyway.

If your cooking's only got two moves—shake and bake—then it's time to mix things up with recipes like Krusty Burgers, Squishees, and Million-Dollar Birthday Fries. From breakfast to dessert and everything in between, it's good old-fashioned home cooking, deep-fried to perfection. (Note: Not everything is deep-fried.)

But before you start cooking, read this thingy that tells you how to work the stuff:

- Some dishes, like fugu fish, are far too diddly-dangerous for home cooks, and some are just too gross, like sixty-four slices of American cheese. While a few of the foods seen on the show are unpossible (like the original Sloppy Jimbos), this book features tasty versions inspired by the look and flavors of the original cartoon eats.

- Always read through a recipe completely before starting to double-check you have the ingredients, equipment, and time needed to finish the dish. Most recipes include variations with shortcuts and flavor tweaks, as well as tips for making the best Simpsons recipes possible. Woo-hoo!

- As you might have guessed, there are some deep-fried recipes in this book (drooling noise). Use a tall heavy pot and an abundance of caution when frying.
- Some recipes call for special equipment like a candy or deep-frying thermometer, stand mixer, or ice cream maker. However, the vast majority of the recipes don't require anything special, and all can be made by beginners and Boyardees alike.
- When measuring flour or cocoa, scoop it into the measuring cup, tap it to settle, and sweep off the excess with a knife. And don't skip greasing your pan or you'll be yelling "d'oh!"
- Feel free to put your own spin on these dishes, but experiment at your own risk. Any changes to recipes beyond the provided variations may cause things to go up in flames like a bowl of cornflakes.

Whether you're fixing Homer's Patented Space-Age Out-of-This-World Moon Waffles while watching episodes with your family on Saturday morning or having a few of your best barfly friends over for White Wine Spritzers, *The Simpsons* is meant to be viewed with food or drink in hand. Try hosting a potluck and let each person choose their own recipe for a viewing and eating marathon that would make Homer proud.

In the immortal words of Marge Simpson, "Sometimes the most satisfying meal is the one you cook yourself." Thank you for choo-choo-choosing this book. You won't believe you ate the whole thing.

CHAPTER 1

BREAKFAST

Never start your day on an empty stomach. Whether you're spending a lazy, sacrilegious Sunday morning making Homer's Patented Space-Age Out-of-This-World Moon Waffles or beginning your workday with the requisite Purple-Filled Doughnut (or dozen), breakfast is the most important meal of the day. Sure, you could always pour a bowl of Jackie O's or Kelp Chex, top it with eggnog, and call it a

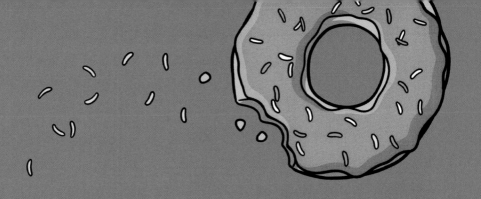

day, but why not use the easy recipes in this chapter to spell out "I love you" with bacon and eggs or cut pancakes into squares? Go the heart-clogging route with a Good Morning Burger or enjoy a bowl of sweet, nourishing Krusty Brand Imitation Gruel. No matter the menu, take a cue from Homer and serve these recipes with plenty of rich, creamery butter.

I LOVE YOU BREAKFAST

 "I Love Lisa," Season 4

Make your huggy bug a hearty breakfast...even if they forgot it was Valentine's Day. Nothing says "I love you" like a plateful of eggs and bacon.

SERVES 1 MEAT-LOVING VALENTINE

6 long slices streaky bacon
1 teaspoon vegetable oil
2 large eggs
Salt and ground black pepper, to taste

1. Line a large rimmed baking sheet with aluminum foil and arrange bacon in a single layer on top. Place in a cold oven and preheat to 400°F. Bake 15 minutes (add or subtract 5 minutes depending on the thickness of the bacon) until crisp. Drain bacon on a large paper towel–lined plate.
2. When bacon is almost finished cooking, add oil to a medium skillet over medium heat. Gently crack eggs into the pan, keeping them separate, without puncturing yolks. Season with salt and pepper. Cook 3–4 minutes or until desired doneness is reached. If needed, cover the pan for 30 seconds–1 minute to cook egg whites through.
3. Cut 4 slices bacon into halves and 2 slices bacon into quarters. Construct the words "I love you" on a large platter using bacon pieces. Leave space for the o's.
4. Add eggs to the platter as the o's and serve immediately.

Cooking Tips

You can fry the bacon in a skillet, but using the oven is a convenient way to cook a lot of bacon at once. Kitchen shears are handy for cutting the cooked bacon. Double the eggs for breakfast for two.

HOMER'S PATENTED SPACE-AGE OUT-OF-THIS-WORLD MOON WAFFLES

 "Homer the Heretic," Season 4

Homer's original waffles include burnt caramels, liquid smoke, and waffle batter wrapped around an entire stick of butter. Mmm...fattening. These buttery waffles with smoky caramel sauce are more presentable and won't wreck your waffle iron.

MAKES 4 WAFFLES

For Caramel Sauce

½ cup granulated sugar
¼ cup (½ stick) salted butter
¾ cup heavy whipping cream, warmed
1 teaspoon vanilla extract
3 or 4 drops liquid smoke

1. To make Caramel Sauce: Add sugar and butter to a large saucepan over medium heat. Melt butter and continue to cook while stirring until mixture turns a deep golden brown and just barely begins to smoke.
2. Immediately remove from heat and very slowly add warm heavy cream, stirring constantly. Add vanilla and liquid smoke and stir. Cover and set aside.

Cooking Tips

If you are using unsalted butter, add a pinch (¹⁄₁₆ teaspoon) of salt to the Caramel Sauce and ¼ teaspoon salt to the waffle batter. Use a bigger saucepan than you think you'll need for the Caramel Sauce since it bubbles up, and don't walk away while making it—it'll suddenly burn before you realize what happened. The sauce will keep for up to a week in a sealed container in the refrigerator. Reheat gently in the microwave or in a heatproof bowl in a pot of hot water and use to top ice cream, cake, and other treats.

Recipe Variations

You can make the waffles without the Caramel Sauce and simply top them with maple syrup. Add a few drops of liquid smoke to the syrup for a smoky flavor.

For Waffles

1½ cups buttermilk
½ cup (1 stick) salted butter, melted
2 large eggs
1 teaspoon vanilla extract
1½ cups all-purpose flour
2 tablespoons cornstarch
2 tablespoons granulated sugar
2 teaspoons baking powder
1 teaspoon baking soda

3. To make Waffles: Whisk together buttermilk, melted butter, eggs, and vanilla in a large bowl. Add flour, cornstarch, sugar, baking powder, and baking soda. Whisk until just combined.

4. Preheat a waffle iron according to manual instructions, lightly greasing with cooking spray or oil if needed. Once hot, add ¼ of the batter and close lid. Cook until waffle is browned and crisp. Repeat with remaining batter.

5. Stir warm Caramel Sauce and drizzle over Waffles. Leave waffle iron for Marge to clean later.

KRUSTY BRAND IMITATION GRUEL

 "Kamp Krusty," Season 4

Sweet, nourishing gruel! It might have an unappetizing gray hue, but homemade gruel is actually a delicious way to start the day. Plus, it has Krusty's seal of approval.

SERVES 4

1 cup uncooked brown rice (long- or short-grain)

4 cups rice milk

3 cups water

¼ teaspoon salt

¾ cup fresh blueberries

¼ cup packed light brown sugar

1 tablespoon freshly ground chia seeds

⅛ teaspoon ground nutmeg

Optional Toppings: More blueberries, brown sugar or maple syrup, cream or yogurt

1. Pulse brown rice in a food processor or blender a few times to break up grains.
2. Combine rice, rice milk, water, and salt in a large saucepan. Bring to a boil over high heat, then reduce the heat to low and simmer. Cook, stirring every 5–10 minutes, about 45 minutes.
3. Add blueberries, brown sugar, chia seeds, and nutmeg and stir. Simmer another 20 minutes, continuing to stir occasionally and mashing blueberries a bit as they cook. Add extra water as needed if gruel becomes too thick. Rice should be very tender when done.
4. Serve warm.

Cooking Tips

The ground chia seeds lend the dish a gray color and some added nutrition. Grind them using a spice grinder, coffee grinder, or mortar and pestle.

Recipe Variations

Any milk will work, including regular milk or other nondairy milks. You can also make this gruel in a slow cooker. Add rice, rice milk, water, and salt; stir; cook on low for 7–8 hours. Add other ingredients and stir well, cooking for another 30 minutes–1 hour.

KENT BROCKMAN'S DANISH

 "Bart Gets Famous," Season 5

If you simply must start every morning with a Danish, then make these quick and easy cinnamon-sugar pastries. Since this recipe makes a big batch, there'll be enough to go around the whole studio lot. Yoink!

MAKES 18 SMALL PASTRIES

6 tablespoons unsalted butter, at room temperature, divided
5 tablespoons granulated sugar
1 teaspoon ground cinnamon
1/4 teaspoon salt
1 (20-ounce) box frozen puff pastry (2 sheets), thawed

1. Preheat oven to 400°F. Line a large rimmed baking sheet with parchment paper and coat with 1 tablespoon butter.
2. Combine sugar, cinnamon, and salt in a small bowl.
3. Sprinkle a clean work surface with about 1½ teaspoons sugar mixture and unfold one puff pastry sheet on top.
4. Roll dough out to a 9" × 12" rectangle. Brush with 2 tablespoons butter, spreading to the edge, and sprinkle with 2 tablespoons sugar mixture, leaving ½" of one 9" side bare.
5. Starting with the shorter end coated in butter and sugar mixture, roll puff pastry into a tight log. Roll log back and forth a few times to seal. Slice into nine 1" pinwheels. Repeat with remaining puff pastry.
6. Sprinkle a little more sugar mixture on the work surface and flatten pinwheels to about ½" tall using your hand or a rolling pin.
7. Evenly space pinwheels on prepared baking sheet with sealed ends turned inward toward one another. Brush with remaining butter and sprinkle with remaining sugar mixture.
8. Bake 20 minutes or until puffed and deep golden brown but not burnt on bottoms.
9. Enjoy warm or at room temperature. Now, that's a Danish.

FORBIDDEN DOUGHNUTS

 "Treehouse of Horror IV," Season 5

So you like doughnuts, eh? Make these easy baked cake doughnuts at home so everyone can enjoy Daddy's soul doughnut. You don't even have to sell your soul to Flanders.

MAKES 15 DOUGHNUTS

For Doughnuts

1½ cups all-purpose flour
1 teaspoon baking powder
½ teaspoon salt
½ cup (1 stick) unsalted butter, at room temperature
¾ cup granulated sugar
½ cup vegetable oil
4 large eggs, yolks and whites separated
1 teaspoon vanilla extract

1. Preheat oven to 375°F. Lightly grease a large doughnut pan with nonstick cooking spray or butter.
2. To make Doughnuts: Sift flour, baking powder, and salt into a large bowl. Set aside.
3. In a separate large bowl, beat butter and sugar together 3 minutes until fluffy. Add oil and beat. Add egg yolks and vanilla and beat 2 minutes or until pale yellow and creamy.
4. Add egg whites to a medium mixing bowl or bowl of a stand mixer. Beat with an electric mixer until soft peaks form.
5. Gently mix flour mixture into butter mixture just until incorporated. Fold in whipped egg whites, being careful to lose as little air as possible from the mixture.
6. Spoon mixture into a large zip-top bag and close. Snip a corner with a pair of scissors, creating a ¾" opening. Fill doughnut molds a little over halfway.
7. Bake 10 minutes or until tops are very lightly golden brown and a toothpick inserted in the middle comes out clean. Let Doughnuts cool 3 minutes in pan before turning out onto a cooling rack.

(continued ▶)

Cooking Tips

Don't over-fill the doughnut pan or you'll lose the signature hole. If you prefer fried yeast doughnuts, use the dough recipe for Purple-Filled Doughnuts (see recipe in this chapter) and cut the dough into a classic doughnut shape using a doughnut cutter. Fry, let cool, and glaze.

For Glaze

- 1½ cups powdered sugar
- 3 tablespoons unsalted butter, melted
- 1 tablespoon whole milk, plus more for thinning
- ½ teaspoon vanilla extract
- Red or pink food coloring
- Rainbow sprinkles

8. Once the Doughnuts are completely cooled (about 1 hour), make Glaze. Add powdered sugar, melted butter, milk, and vanilla to a small mixing bowl and mix well. Add food coloring a drop at a time until desired color is reached. Add more milk if needed, a little at a time, until Glaze is thin enough for dipping but opaque and thick enough to stay on Doughnuts without running too much.

9. Dip 1 Doughnut in Glaze halfway and spin slowly as you pull it out. Turn it right side up and place it back on the cooling rack. Repeat dipping with remaining Doughnuts, decorating with sprinkles as you go. Serve.

REVEREND LOVEJOY'S STIGMUFFINS

 "Insane Clown Poppy," Season 12

From the Festival of Books release *Someone's in the Kitchen with Jesus,* Reverend Lovejoy's Stigmuffins are to die for. They're a classic banana muffin with a macabre religious twist.

MAKES 12 MUFFINS

1½ cups all-purpose flour
1½ teaspoons baking powder
1 teaspoon ground cinnamon
½ teaspoon baking soda
½ teaspoon salt
3 large very ripe bananas, peeled and mashed
⅔ cup plus 2 tablespoons granulated sugar, divided
⅓ cup vegetable oil
1 large egg
1 teaspoon vanilla extract
Optional: ½ cup chopped walnuts

1. Preheat oven to 350°F. Lightly grease a twelve-cup muffin pan with nonstick cooking spray or line with cupcake liners.
2. Mix together flour, baking powder, cinnamon, baking soda, and salt in a small mixing bowl.
3. Add bananas, ⅔ cup sugar, oil, egg, and vanilla to a separate medium mixing bowl. Whisk together until well combined.
4. Add dry ingredients and nuts (if using) to wet ingredients and gently mix until just combined. Fill each muffin cup ⅔ full. Sprinkle with remaining sugar.
5. Bake 20 minutes or until a toothpick inserted in the middle comes out clean.
6. Let muffins cool 5 minutes before turning out onto a cooling rack.
7. Use a small tall circle cutter or boba straw to cut out the center of each muffin.

Recipe Variations

Swap the nuts for chocolate chips, or add a handful of chopped dates along with the nuts for extra sweetness and texture.

AGNES SKINNER'S PRESERVES

 "Bart the Murderer," Season 3

These delicious preserves will keep you going, whether you're desperately licking them out of the jar from under a stack of old newspapers or slathering them on toast or biscuits.

MAKES 16 OUNCES

1 pound fresh raspberries, blackberries, or hulled strawberries (or a mix)

$2/3$ cup granulated sugar

2 tablespoons lemon juice

1 pinch ($1/16$ teaspoon) salt

1 long piece lemon peel, including white pith

1. Place three metal spoons in the freezer (retrieve any extra spoons at end if not needed).
2. Add berries, sugar, lemon juice, and salt to a large saucepan. Mash roughly with a potato masher or fork until well combined. Add lemon peel.
3. Stir over low heat to dissolve sugar. Bring to a boil and boil 18 minutes, stirring frequently, until mixture is thickening up and darker in color and bubbles are smaller.
4. Retrieve one spoon from freezer and dip it in preserves, then remove it. Let it cool 1 second before running your finger through the jam on the back of the spoon. If it leaves a clean trail that doesn't run into the middle, it's done. If it's not quite set up, boil a few minutes more and test again.
5. Remove preserves from heat and discard lemon peel. Transfer preserves to one clean pint jar or two clean half-pint jars and cap.
6. Store preserves in the refrigerator up to 1 month closed and up to 3 weeks once opened.

Recipe Variations

Small amounts of extra ingredients can add lots of flavor to these preserves. Try adding a little vanilla, a spice like cardamom, or a touch of berry liqueur like framboise after boiling. You can also add up to an extra $1/3$ cup sugar for more sweetness.

LUMBERJACK BREAKFAST

 "Dead Putting Society," Season 2

If you're not a racehorse on a strict diet of complex carbohydrates, this high-protein steak-and-egg breakfast will give you the energy to win the day.

SERVES 2

1 (12-ounce) sirloin steak, 1" thick
Kosher salt, to taste
2 teaspoons vegetable oil, divided
1 tablespoon butter
Ground black pepper, to taste
4 large eggs
Optional Toppings: Steak sauce or
    hot sauce

1. Season steak on both sides with salt and let rest at room temperature 30 minutes.
2. Preheat a large cast iron skillet over medium heat 5 minutes, then increase heat to medium-high. Use a paper towel to dry steak on both sides.
3. Add 1 teaspoon oil to the pan, followed by steak. Cook without moving 4 minutes or until a nice crust forms.
4. Flip steak and place butter on top. Reduce heat to medium. Once butter melts, tilt the pan and baste steak with butter, careful to avoid hot splatters from the pan. Check doneness after 5 minutes. Medium-rare will register 130°F and medium will register 140°F.
5. Remove steak to a large plate and season with pepper. Tent with aluminum foil and let rest while cooking eggs.
6. Heat remaining 1 teaspoon oil in a separate medium skillet over medium heat. Carefully crack eggs into the skillet. Season with salt and pepper. Cook 3–4 minutes or until desired doneness.
7. Slice steak against the grain and serve alongside eggs on two large plates. Eat your steak, boy.

SQUARE PANCAKES

 "Treehouse of Horror VII," Season 8

If your waffle iron is in the shop, there's only one solution: Make Square Pancakes. These light and fluffy pancakes are so delicious, no one (except Lisa) will notice they're not waffles.

SERVES 4

1¾ cups all-purpose flour
1 tablespoon granulated sugar
2 teaspoons baking powder
½ teaspoon salt
1¾ cups buttermilk
2 large eggs
2 tablespoons vegetable oil
Toppings: Butter, syrup

1. Combine flour, sugar, baking powder, and salt in a medium mixing bowl. Add buttermilk, eggs, and oil and mix until just combined. Let batter sit 10 minutes while you prepare toppings and heat pan.
2. Heat a large skillet or griddle over medium heat. Once hot, grease lightly with butter. Add about ½ cup batter to make a large pancake, quickly but gently coaxing it into a square-like shape.
3. Cook 3 minutes or until bubbles are rising and popping throughout batter and pancake is golden brown on bottom. Flip and cook 2 minutes or until cooked through and browned on the other side.
4. Remove pancake to a large plate and lightly grease skillet again. Repeat with remaining batter to make 6–8 large pancakes.
5. Use a large knife to trim the sides to make each pancake into a perfect square. Serve with butter and syrup and tell your family they're waffles.

Cooking Tips

The trimmed edges of these pancakes are fun to eat and a good snack for kids. Simply dunk them in syrup and enjoy.

GOOD MORNING BURGERS

 "Bart's Friend Falls in Love," Season 3

Topped with bacon, ham, a fried egg, and a rich, creamery butter hollandaise sauce, these Good Morning Burgers are drool-inducing.

SERVES 2

¾ pound 80% ground beef
Kosher salt and ground black pepper, to taste
2 egg yolks
1 teaspoon lemon juice
¼ cup (½ stick) butter, melted and warm
4 slices thick-cut bacon
2 large eggs
2 hamburger buns, toasted
2 slices cooked thick-cut ham, warmed

1. Form ground beef into 2 patties almost 1" wider than buns. Season with salt and pepper and make a shallow indent in the middle of each patty to make the centers slightly thinner than the edges. Chill in the refrigerator while you prepare other ingredients.

2. Whisk together egg yolks and lemon juice in a small heatproof bowl that will fit over a small saucepan. Add about 1" water to the pan and bring it to a simmer over medium heat. Place bowl over water and whisk egg mixture until foamy.

3. Slowly add melted butter while whisking vigorously. Whisk until creamy and thickened. Turn heat down to low and keep sauce warm, whisking occasionally and adding a sprinkle of water if it becomes too thick.

4. Add bacon to a large skillet over medium heat. Cook until bacon reaches desired crispness, about 10 minutes, turning once halfway through. Remove bacon from pan, leaving grease, and place on a medium paper towel–lined plate. Increase heat under skillet to medium-high.

(continued ▶)

5. Add burger patties to skillet and cook 5 minutes or until browned and slightly crispy on bottom. Flip and cook another 5 minutes or until they reach desired doneness (patty should have an internal temperature of at least 145°F for medium well-done). Remove to a medium plate. Reduce heat under skillet to medium.

6. Crack remaining 2 eggs into the skillet, being careful to keep them separate and keep yolks whole. Season with salt and pepper. Cook about 3–4 minutes or until whites are cooked but yolks are runny. If needed, cover pan 30 seconds–1 minute to cook egg whites through.

7. Place burger patties atop toasted bottom buns. Spoon hollandaise sauce on each burger and top with equal amounts ham, bacon, and fried eggs. Add top buns. Call them Good Morning Burgers and eat them.

PURPLE-FILLED DOUGHNUTS

 "Homer Defined," Season 3

Mmm...purple. You can enjoy these doughnuts guilt-free because they're filled with purple stuff and purple's a fruit!

MAKES 15 DOUGHNUTS

1 cup lukewarm whole milk

½ cup granulated sugar, divided

1 (¼-ounce) packet active dry yeast

1 large egg

3 tablespoons unsalted butter, melted, then cooled slightly

½ teaspoon vanilla extract

3 cups all-purpose flour, plus extra for dusting

½ teaspoon salt

1 quart canola oil

1 cup blackberry jelly

1. Combine milk, ¼ cup sugar, and yeast in the bowl of a stand mixer or a large mixing bowl. Let sit 5 minutes until it starts to foam.

2. Add egg, melted butter, and vanilla and whisk. Add flour and salt and mix on low speed or with a wooden spoon. If dough is too sticky to handle, add more flour a little at a time.

3. Knead dough 6 minutes by hand on a lightly floured clean surface, or using the dough hook on a stand mixer, until smooth and elastic. Add a little flour as needed (dough should feel sticky but not actively stick to the surface or your hands).

4. Place dough in a large oiled bowl, cover, and let rise in a warm place 1 hour or until doubled in size.

5. Punch down dough and place on a lightly floured clean surface. Roll out dough with a rolling pin until slightly under ½" thick. Use a 3" round cutter and cut out 15 circles. Discard excess. Cover circles loosely with a towel and let rise 30 minutes.

6. Line a large baking sheet with paper towels. Add 1" oil to a large heavy-bottomed pot and heat over medium-high heat to 350°F.

(continued ▷)

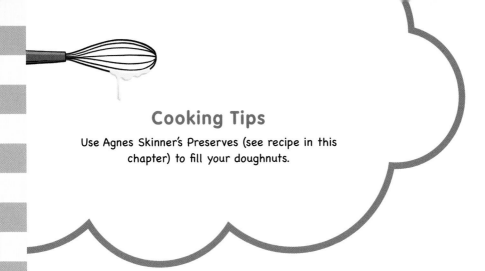

Cooking Tips

Use Agnes Skinner's Preserves (see recipe in this chapter) to fill your doughnuts.

7. Once oil is hot, carefully add 5 doughnuts at a time with a slotted spatula and fry 2 minutes on one side, or until deep golden brown. Flip and fry another 1 minute or so, until just browned on the other side. Remove to the prepared baking sheet to drain.
8. Repeat frying and draining with remaining dough. Roll still-warm doughnuts in remaining ¼ cup sugar and let cool about 15 minutes.
9. Add a large round or star tip to a pastry bag or a zip-top bag with a corner cut out. Add jelly to the bag and seal it. Poke each doughnut with a skewer or chopstick, then press the tip halfway into the side of each doughnut and squeeze in jelly until it dribbles out. Serve immediately.

CHAPTER 2

LUNCH

Quit nursing that leftover 10' hoagie and make yourself some lunch that won't turn your lips blue. While you could eat whatever slop Lunchlady Doris has prepared or stick a rice cake diet sandwich in the microwave, it's worth the effort for the homemade Maude's Club Sandwich and School Lunch Tater Tots in the following chapter. Or make your very own Krusty Burgers and pass them off as steamed hams, but be warned: Loneliness and cheeseburgers are a dangerous mix. There are even a few vegetarian options in this chapter (like Lisa's Gazpacho) if you don't want to have a cow, man.

KRUSTY BURGERS

 "22 Short Films about Springfield," Season 7

At your next luncheon, impress your guests with these delicious steamed hams (it's an Albany expression). Despite the fact that they are obviously grilled, these hamburgers are definitely *not* from Krusty Burger.

SERVES 6

2 pounds 80% ground beef

2 medium garlic cloves, peeled and minced

1½ teaspoons kosher salt

¾ teaspoon ground black pepper

Optional: ½ teaspoon onion powder

½ cup mayonnaise

2 tablespoons ketchup

1 tablespoon pickle relish, sweet or dill

2 teaspoons pickle juice

2 teaspoons mustard

Optional: 6 slices cheese

6 hamburger buns

Optional Toppings: Shredded lettuce, 12 sliced dill pickles

1. Add ground beef, garlic, salt, pepper, and onion powder (if using) to a large mixing bowl. Fold together using your hands until just combined.
2. Form mixture into 6 burger patties. Make patties almost 1" wider than buns, pressing the middle of each patty to make the center slightly thinner than the edges. Place patties on a large plate in the refrigerator to chill uncovered while you heat the grill and make sauce.
3. Preheat a clean grill to 450°F.
4. In a small mixing bowl, combine mayonnaise, ketchup, pickle relish, pickle juice, and mustard. Cover and store in the refrigerator until ready to use.
5. Once the grill is hot, lightly oil the grates. Remove patties from the refrigerator and add to the grill. Cook about 3 minutes or until browned on one side with visible grill marks.
6. Flip patties and cook 5 more minutes or to preferred doneness (patty should have an internal temperature of at least 145°F for medium well-done). If you're making cheeseburgers, add cheese in the last minute of grilling.
7. Let burgers rest 2 minutes on large plates. If desired, briefly toast the buns.
8. Add sauce to both sides of buns. Top with patties, followed by toppings. Serve on a silver platter.

Cooking Tips

The sauce will keep for at least a week in the refrigerator. Serve these burgers with Million-Dollar Birthday Fries (see recipe in Chapter 3).

IRS-WICHES

If you're not quite in the mood for tax burgers, go for an IRS-wich. By making your own grilled chicken sandwich at home, you don't have to wait 6–8 weeks or deduct your gambling losses. Feel free to withhold the lettuce.

SERVES 4

2 cups cool water
2 tablespoons kosher salt
4 (4-ounce) boneless, skinless
  chicken breast cutlets
4 medium garlic cloves, peeled and
  smashed
1 tablespoon vegetable oil, plus
  more for grilling
Ground black pepper, to taste
4 hamburger buns, toasted
Optional Toppings: Lettuce, sliced
  tomato, sliced onion, mayonnaise

1. Add water and salt to a small casserole dish or loaf pan and stir until salt is dissolved. Add chicken breasts and garlic. Breasts should be covered by brine. Place in the refrigerator 45 minutes–1 hour.
2. Remove brined chicken from the refrigerator and drain. Pat dry with paper towels. Coat on all sides with oil and season with pepper.
3. Preheat a clean grill to about 375°F. Lightly oil the grates.
4. Add prepared chicken breasts to the hot grill. Grill about 3 minutes or until grill marks form and edges turn opaque. Flip chicken and close the lid. Grill another 4 minutes or until cooked through and internal temperature is 165°F.
5. Remove chicken from the grill and let it rest on a large plate while toasting buns and preparing toppings. Assemble sandwiches and serve with a dependent-sized soda.

Cooking Tips

Look for thinly sliced chicken breast cutlets about 1/2" thick. If you have regular chicken breasts, you can use a sharp knife to slice them in half lengthwise, turning two large chicken breasts into four thin pieces that are perfect for sandwiches.

LISA'S GAZPACHO

 "Lisa the Vegetarian," Season 7

Gazpacho is tomato soup, served ice-cold! And while it might make some barbecue attendees groan, it's refreshing and satisfying on a hot day. The smooth texture and balanced flavor might even win over some meat lovers.

SERVES 6

2 pounds ripe heirloom tomatoes, cored and chopped

1 large red bell pepper, seeded and chopped

1 large cucumber, peeled, seeded, and chopped

1 small bunch green onions, trimmed and sliced, whites and greens separated

1 medium garlic clove, peeled and chopped

1 teaspoon red wine vinegar

Salt and ground black pepper, to taste

$\frac{1}{2}$ cup plus 1 tablespoon extra-virgin olive oil, divided

$\frac{1}{3}$ cup packed fresh basil leaves, finely chopped

1 small jalapeño pepper, seeded and minced

Zest of 1 medium lemon

1. Add tomatoes, bell pepper, cucumber, white parts of green onions, garlic, vinegar, and $\frac{1}{8}$ teaspoon each salt and pepper to a blender.
2. Process until smooth and well blended. If needed, blend in batches.
3. With the blender running on low speed, drizzle in $\frac{1}{2}$ cup oil. Strain purée through a fine-mesh strainer, using a wooden spoon or rubber spatula to push mixture through the strainer, and discard pulp. Chill in the refrigerator at least 1 hour.
4. Combine green onion tops, basil, jalapeño, and lemon zest in a small bowl and season with salt and pepper. Add remaining 1 tablespoon oil and toss.
5. Serve soup ice-cold in small bowls or chilled cups topped with basil mixture.

MONKEY PAW TURKEY SANDWICHES

 "Treehouse of Horror II," Season 3

This sandwich is free of zombie turkeys, won't turn you into a turkey, and has no other weird surprises. It's not even a little bit dry!

SERVES 4

1 (3-pound) bone-in, skin-on turkey breast
1 tablespoon kosher salt
1 teaspoon packed light brown sugar
1 teaspoon smoked or sweet paprika
½ teaspoon ground black pepper
¼ teaspoon garlic powder
8 slices rye bread, lightly toasted
Toppings: Hot mustard (to taste), 4 large leaves lettuce, 4–8 slices tomato

1. Pat turkey breast dry with paper towels. Combine salt, brown sugar, paprika, pepper, and garlic powder in a small bowl and rub onto turkey breast, covering all sides and under skin. Wrap turkey in plastic wrap and let brine in the refrigerator about 12 hours.
2. Remove turkey from the refrigerator 30 minutes before roasting. Preheat oven to 400°F.
3. Pat turkey dry with paper towels and place in a small roasting pan lined with aluminum foil or in a large ovenproof skillet. Place in the oven and reduce temperature to 325°F.
4. Start checking after 1 hour and remove turkey from the oven when a thermometer inserted in the thickest part of breast reads 160°F.
5. Cover loosely with foil and let rest at least 30 minutes before slicing.
6. Remove skin and cut breast from bone. Slice breast meat into thin slices.
7. Add hot mustard to taste on 4 slices rye bread. Top with lettuce, tomato, and roasted turkey, followed by remaining bread slices. Be satisfied that you got your wish and there weren't any weird surprises.

Cooking Tips

If you have a smaller breast or a boneless turkey breast, it will take less time to cook. Start checking after 45 minutes.

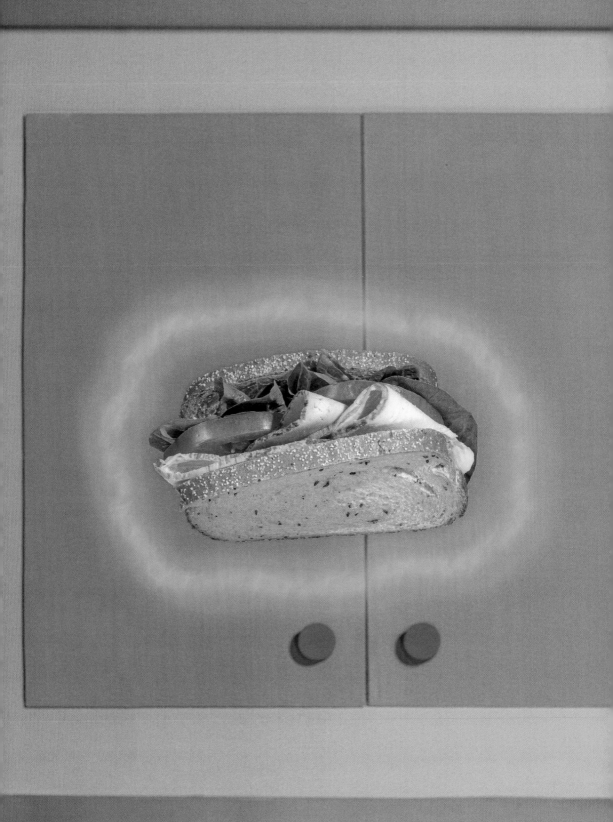

SCHOOL LUNCH TATER TOTS

 "Principal Charming," Season 2

For the best Tater Tots money can buy, take matters into your own hands. Even Principal Skinner will swear off cafeteria food after tasting this homemade version.

SERVES 6

2 pounds russet potatoes, peeled and cut into 2" slices
½ medium yellow onion, peeled and grated
1 tablespoon cornstarch
1 teaspoon kosher salt
1 teaspoon garlic powder
½ teaspoon ground black pepper
1½ quarts canola oil

1. Bring a large pot of water to a boil over high heat. Add potatoes and cook about 15 minutes, until a sharp knife pierces a potato halfway through but with some resistance.

2. Drain potatoes and let cool 5 minutes in a colander. While potatoes cool, use your hands to squeeze any liquid out of grated onion and add it to a large mixing bowl.

3. Once cool enough to handle, grate cooked potato slices using a box grater or grater attachment on a food processor. Add to the bowl with onion.

4. Add cornstarch, salt, garlic powder, and pepper. Using your hands, toss to combine, making sure dry ingredients are well distributed.

5. Add oil to a large deep heavy-bottomed pan and heat to 350°F over medium-high heat.

6. While oil is heating, grab about ¼ of the potato mixture and place it on a clean surface. Press it together as you coax it into a long log about 1" wide. Cut log into 1½" pieces, using your hands to smooth the ends of the cut pieces. Repeat with remaining mixture.

7. Fry potato pieces in oil in four batches until deep golden brown and crisp, about 5 minutes per batch, stirring once or twice to make sure they don't stick to the bottom.

8. Use a slotted spoon or spider to remove cooked Tater Tots from oil. Drain on a cooling rack or large paper towel–lined plate and let cool 5 minutes before digging in. Serve on a school lunch tray.

Cooking Tips

Fried and cooled School Lunch Tater Tots can be frozen. Place on a large parchment paper–lined baking sheet and freeze for 1 hour, then add to a zip-top bag and store for up to 1 month. To reheat, place frozen pieces on a large baking sheet and bake in a preheated 400°F oven for 10–15 minutes.

MOE'S HOBO CHICKEN CHILI

 "Bart Sells His Soul," Season 7

Skip the bottom-feeding suction eel and try Moe's Hobo Chicken Chili. This recipe starts with the best part of the chicken—the thigh—and adds secret hobo spices. *Très bien!*

SERVES 4

1 tablespoon extra-virgin olive oil
1 small yellow onion, peeled and diced
1 medium bell pepper, seeded and diced
1 small jalapeño pepper, seeded and diced
2 medium garlic cloves, peeled and minced
1 pound boneless, skinless chicken thighs
1 teaspoon chili powder
1 teaspoon ground cumin
1 teaspoon dried oregano
1 pinch ($1/16$ teaspoon) cayenne pepper
1 bay leaf
2 cups chicken broth
1 (7-ounce) can salsa verde
2 (15-ounce) cans white or pinto beans, rinsed and drained
Salt and ground black pepper, to taste
Optional Toppings: Sour cream, diced avocado, fresh cilantro, lime wedges

1. Preheat a large heavy-bottomed pot over medium heat. Add oil followed by onion. Sauté 3 minutes. Add bell pepper, jalapeño, and garlic and sauté 3 more minutes or until onion is mostly translucent.

2. Add chicken, chili powder, cumin, oregano, and cayenne. Stir and cook about 1 minute, until fragrant. Add bay leaf, chicken broth, and salsa verde and stir.

3. Bring to a low simmer and cook 30 minutes, until chicken is tender and internal temperature is at least 165°F. Remove chicken to a plate. Discard bay leaf.

4. Add beans to soup. Shred chicken and add it back to the pot. Simmer 10 more minutes.

5. Taste and add salt and black pepper as needed before serving.

SLOPPY JIMBOS

 "Treehouse of Horror V," Season 6

No Jimbos were harmed in the making of this recipe, but these sandwiches are still young and impudent. Try not to overindulge or you'll end up fat, soft, tender...and sent to detention.

SERVES 6

1 pound lean ground beef
1 small yellow onion, peeled and finely diced
½ medium bell pepper, seeded and finely diced
2 medium garlic cloves, peeled and minced
1 (8-ounce) can tomato sauce
½ cup ketchup
¼ cup water
1 tablespoon Worcestershire sauce
2 teaspoons yellow mustard
1 teaspoon packed light or dark brown sugar
Salt and ground black pepper, to taste
Optional: Hot sauce, to taste
6 hamburger buns

1. Heat a large skillet over medium heat. Add ground beef and cook, breaking up chunks, until browned, about 5 minutes. Using a slotted spoon, remove beef to a large paper towel–lined plate and drain most of the grease from the pan.
2. Return pan to heat. Add onion and bell pepper and cook 3 minutes or until onion is translucent. Add garlic and cook 1 more minute.
3. Add cooked beef, tomato sauce, ketchup, water, Worcestershire sauce, mustard, and brown sugar to pan. Stir and bring to a simmer. Turn the heat to low and simmer 10 minutes.
4. Add salt, black pepper, and hot sauce (if using). If desired, toast the buns.
5. Spoon beef mixture onto buns and serve. *Das ist gut, nein?*

Recipe Variations

This recipe also works well with ground pork, ground turkey, or cooked green or brown lentils instead of ground beef.

FRIED FISH SANDWICHES

 "King-Size Homer," Season 7

Looking to put on some pounds so you can finally work from home? This sandwich is your window to weight gain! Crispy and topped with a homemade tartar sauce, it's worth the calories.

SERVES 4

½ cup mayonnaise
2 tablespoons pickle relish
1 tablespoon minced red onion
2 teaspoons finely chopped fresh parsley
1 teaspoon fresh lemon juice
Salt and ground black pepper, to taste
½ cup all-purpose flour
1 teaspoon smoked or sweet paprika
¼ teaspoon cayenne pepper
2 large eggs, beaten
1 tablespoon water
1¼ cups panko bread crumbs
⅔ pound white fish fillets, cut into 4 pieces
2 cups canola oil
4 potato or brioche hamburger buns
Toppings: 4 medium leaves lettuce, 4 slices tomato

1. In a small mixing bowl, combine mayonnaise, relish, onion, parsley, and lemon juice to make tartar sauce. Season with salt and black pepper. Mix and refrigerate covered until ready to use.
2. Combine flour, paprika, and cayenne in a small bowl and season with salt and black pepper. Add eggs and water to another small bowl. Add panko to a third small bowl and season with salt and black pepper.
3. Working with 1 fillet at a time, coat fish completely in flour mixture and shake off excess. Coat in egg mixture, then let it drain before coating in panko. Repeat with remaining fillets.
4. Heat oil in a large heavy-bottomed skillet over medium-high heat. When hot, drop a piece of breading in. If it starts sizzling right away but doesn't pop or burn, oil is ready. If breading burns, reduce heat and let oil cool a bit before testing again.
5. Let any excess breading fall off 2 fillets, then fry fillets in oil 3 minutes per side or until browned, crispy, and cooked through. Drain on a large paper towel–lined plate and repeat with remaining fillets.
6. Spread tartar sauce on top and bottom buns. Add a fried fish fillet to each bottom bun and top with lettuce, tomato, and top bun.

Cooking Tips

Any firm white fish will work, such as flounder, cod, halibut, or pollack. The homemade tartar sauce can be made ahead of time. Leftover sauce will keep up to 3 days in the refrigerator.

ISOTOPE DOG SUPREMES

 "Hungry, Hungry Homer," Season 12

When it's time to break your hunger strike, do it with a hot dog topped with bold, flavorful Southwestern ingredients.

SERVES 6

1 small ripe mango, peeled, pitted, and finely diced

1 heaping tablespoon minced red onion

Optional: 1 tablespoon chopped fresh cilantro

Juice of ½ small lime

Salt and ground black pepper, to taste

2 small jalapeño peppers, seeded and finely diced

1 medium garlic clove, peeled and minced

2 teaspoons white or apple cider vinegar

1 tablespoon butter

1 large sweet onion, peeled and diced

¼ cup beef broth, pilsner, or water

2 teaspoons mesquite grill seasoning

6 hot dogs

6 hot dog buns

1. In a small bowl, combine diced mango, red onion, cilantro (if using), and lime juice. Season with salt and black pepper and toss. Cover and chill until serving time.

2. Add jalapeños, garlic, and vinegar to a separate small bowl and mix. Season with salt. Cover and chill. If grilling hot dogs, preheat grill.

3. Add butter to a large cast iron skillet. Melt on stovetop over medium heat, then add sweet onion and stir. Cook, stirring occasionally, 7 minutes or until onion is translucent. Add broth and mesquite seasoning and stir. Reduce heat to low and simmer 20 minutes or until onion is tender and most of the liquid has evaporated.

4. Grill, bake, or panfry hot dogs until plumped and browned on all sides. Toast buns if desired.

5. Add a hot dog to each bun. Top with sweet onion, chilled relish, and salsa. The truth never tasted so good.

Cooking Tips

The toppings can be made up to a day ahead of time and stored covered in the refrigerator.

MAUDE'S CLUB SANDWICH

 "Dead Putting Society," Season 2

Club sandwiches cut into cute wedges are a nice snack for hungry boys, especially when served with a mug of beer. This recipe is easy to double or triple for a party (or if you invited a hungry Homer over).

**MAKES 1 SANDWICH
(4 WEDGES)**

4 large slices bacon

3 large slices sandwich bread, crusts trimmed

3 tablespoons mayonnaise

2 large leaves lettuce

2 thick slices deli turkey

2 slices vine-ripe tomato

2 thick slices deli ham

1. Add bacon to a large skillet and turn heat to medium. Cook until crispy, about 10 minutes, turning once halfway through cooking. Remove to a large paper towel–lined plate to drain.
2. Lightly toast bread on one side. Apply mayonnaise to toasted sides.
3. Add 1 lettuce leaf and turkey followed by bacon to the mayonnaise side of one bread slice. Top second bread slice, on the mayonnaise side, with 1 lettuce leaf, tomato, and ham. Stack one on top of the other and top with last bread slice, mayonnaise side down.
4. Slice into four triangles and spear with extra-long fancy toothpicks. Serve.

Cooking Tips

Dress up your club sandwich with avocado mayonnaise:
Add $1/2$ of a large ripe avocado to a bowl and mash until creamy.
Add 1 heaping tablespoon of mayonnaise, a squeeze of fresh lemon juice, and a sprinkle of salt and pepper. Mix well and spread on your sandwich in place of the plain mayonnaise.

PRETTY EXCITING CELERY SOUP

 "The Springfield Connection," Season 6

This creamy celery soup is way more delicious than it sounds. It'll make you want to jump in the air and yell, "*Marge!*"

SERVES 4

¼ cup (½ stick) butter

1 medium bunch celery, trimmed and chopped

1 medium white or yellow onion, peeled and diced

1 pound white or yellow potatoes, peeled and cubed

2 medium garlic cloves, peeled and minced

Salt and ground black pepper, to taste

3½ cups chicken or vegetable broth

¼ cup plus 2 teaspoons chopped fresh parsley, divided

¼ cup sour cream or plain Greek yogurt

1. Add butter to a soup pot or large saucepan over medium heat. Once melted, add celery and onion and sauté about 7 minutes or until onion is translucent. Add potatoes and garlic and stir. Season with salt and pepper.
2. Add broth and bring to a boil. Reduce heat to medium-low and simmer about 20 minutes or until potatoes and celery are very tender. Remove from heat.
3. Add ¼ cup parsley and sour cream and stir. Use an immersion blender to purée soup until very smooth, or add to a blender (in batches if needed) and blend. If using a stand blender, leave the top cracked and cover with a kitchen towel.
4. Serve hot garnished with remaining 2 teaspoons parsley.

Recipe Variations

For a greener hue, add more fresh herbs or fresh spinach at the end of cooking and stir until just wilted before puréeing. Swap some of the onion for leeks or replace potatoes with cauliflower for a low-carb option.

RIBWICHES

 "I'm Spelling As Fast As I Can," Season 14

If you're getting the shakes (and getting the fries), it's time for a Ribwich. This homemade sandwich will turn you into a cross-country Ribhead.

SERVES 4

3 pounds (1–2 racks) pork baby back ribs, membrane removed
1 tablespoon kosher salt
2 teaspoons packed light or dark brown sugar
2 teaspoons smoked or sweet paprika
1 teaspoon ground cumin
1 teaspoon ground black pepper
1 teaspoon garlic powder
½ teaspoon cayenne pepper
¾ cup barbecue sauce, divided
4 French rolls, split and lightly toasted
Toppings: 12 sliced pickles, 12 thin slices white onion

1. Preheat oven to 325°F. Line a large rimmed baking sheet with aluminum foil.
2. Use a knife to lightly score through the fat down the center of each pork rib. Place on the prepared baking sheet, bone side down.
3. Combine salt, brown sugar, paprika, cumin, black pepper, garlic powder, and cayenne in a small bowl. Coat ribs with seasoning on all sides.
4. Cover baking sheet tightly with aluminum foil. Bake until ribs are tender and internal temperature is at least 145°F, about 2 hours. Uncover and let cool about 30 minutes, until cool enough to handle.
5. Flip ribs over so they are bone side up. Carefully remove bones, pulling them up through the scoring made before cooking. Discard bones and preheat broiler to high.
6. Cut rack(s) into four equal pieces. Flip them over using a spatula and top pieces with ⅓ cup barbecue sauce. Broil about 5 minutes or until browned and slightly crisped but not burnt.
7. Add remaining barbecue sauce to rolls. Transfer ribs to rolls topped with pickles and onions (if using). You won't mind the taste!

CHAPTER 3

SNACKS

Let's all go to the lobby and get ourselves some snacks! For a quick bite, you *could* grab a bag of Chippos or a can of Nuts and Gum (together at last!), but if you're looking for something a little more substantial that's fit for a party, the recipes in this chapter will do the trick. For a fun appetizer, throw together

56

one of Marge's snack platters or some of Bart's America Balls. For a snack worthy of the big game, construct your very own Nacho Hat and fill it with cheese dip. With these tasty bites, you'll be ready when the snacking hour strikes.

MARGE'S PATENTED HAPPY CRACKER SNACK PLATTER

 "Homer's Phobia," Season 8

If you like your beer cold, your TV loud, and your snacks smiling, then whip up Marge's Patented Happy Cracker Snack Platter. It's perfect for a party, especially if your guests work hard and play hard.

SERVES 4

1 sleeve buttery round crackers
1 can spray cheese
1 small jar sliced green olives with pimentos, drained

Make a cheese smile on a cracker. Add a pimento nose and two olive slices for eyes. Repeat with remaining crackers. Voilà!

Cooking Tips

If using whole olives, slice several into round slices and chop the pimentos into little squares.

Recipe Variations

It's easy to replace some of the ingredients to make your own take on the snack platter. Tomatoes, carrots, cucumbers, bell peppers, radishes, and other vegetables cut into small cubes make good noses or even eyes. Capers and nuts can also stand in for eyes or noses. A slice of pickled red onion makes a nice nondairy smile. If you're not a fan of canned cheese, try topping the crackers with your favorite spreadable cheese (like goat cheese, beer cheese, or cream cheese).

POWERSAUCE BARS

 "King of the Hill," Season 9

Unleash the awesome power of apples! Powersauce Bars will give you the energy you need to *almost* scale a mountain.

MAKES 10 BARS

1 cup pitted dates
½ cup toasted whole almonds
1 cup rolled oats
⅓ cup almond flour
½ teaspoon ground cinnamon
½ teaspoon salt
1 cup chopped dried apples
3 tablespoons vegetable oil
2 tablespoons apple butter or applesauce
1 tablespoon honey
1 egg white

1. Preheat oven to 350°F. Line an 8" square baking pan with parchment paper, leaving some overhang to help remove bars.
2. Add dates to a food processor and process until they begin to form a paste. Add almonds and pulse a few times to very roughly chop.
3. Add oats, almond flour, cinnamon, and salt and pulse a few more times to break up oats a bit and mix.
4. Add dried apples, oil, apple butter, honey, and egg white. Pulse a few times until mixture just starts to come together.
5. Press mixture into the prepared pan in an even, well-packed layer. Bake about 25 minutes or until edges are golden brown and the middle is cooked.
6. Let cool in pan about 10 minutes. Use parchment paper to carefully and quickly lift bar mixture out of the pan and set on a cooling rack to cool completely, about 1 hour.
7. Cut into 10 bars using a sharp knife. Store bars in an airtight container at room temperature for up to 3 days.

Cooking Tips

To toast the almonds, spread them out on an unlined baking sheet and bake for about 10 minutes in an oven preheated to 350°F.

NACHOS, FLANDERS-STYLE

 "Home Sweet Homediddly-Dum-Doodily," Season 7

It will come as no surprise that the man who loves white bread with a glass of water on the side (for dippin') has a bland recipe for nachos. But just because Ned likes his food on the simple side doesn't mean you can't dress up this recipe. Add a little spice or swap the cottage cheese with a more flavorful topping.

MAKES 24 "NACHOS"

1 hothouse cucumber, sliced into
   ¼" slices
½ cup plain cottage cheese
Salt and ground black pepper,
   to taste

Top each cucumber slice with a dollop of cottage cheese. Season with salt and pepper. Serve immediately to sheltered, excited children and worldly, incredibly disappointed children.

Cooking Tips

For a quick tuna salad to swap for the cottage cheese, combine 1 can drained white tuna, 3 tablespoons mayonnaise, 1 tablespoon minced yellow onion, 1 teaspoon mustard, and ⅛ teaspoon each salt and pepper. Mix well with a fork, adding more mayonnaise as needed to make the mixture creamy.

Recipe Variations

Try any of these twists: Season with a sprinkle of paprika, add a drizzle of hot sauce, top with pieces of crispy bacon, mix minced jalapeño into the cottage cheese, or swap the cottage cheese with pimento cheese or tuna or crab salad (don't tell Ned; he might faint).

MILLION-DOLLAR BIRTHDAY FRIES

 "Bart Sells His Soul," Season 7

This'll be a treat! You'll get so excited when you make these Million-Dollar Birthday Fries that you'll just have to celebrate.

SERVES 4

2 pounds russet potatoes, sliced into
   ⅓"-thick sticks
6 cups canola oil
Salt, to taste

1. Fill a medium mixing bowl halfway with cool water. Add in potatoes and agitate them in the water to draw out the starch. Drain water and repeat two more times. Drain well.
2. Use paper towels to dry potatoes completely before placing them in a large heavy-bottomed pot. Line a large baking sheet with paper towels and set it near the stovetop.
3. Pour oil into the pot, covering potatoes with 1" oil.
4. Bring oil to a simmer over medium-low heat, then reduce heat to low. Keep at a very low simmer with just a few small bubbles rising about 25 minutes or until fries are tender. Don't stir unless fries are sticking to pot, and only stir once or twice total.
5. Turn heat up to medium-high and cook another 20 minutes or until fries are lightly golden and crisp. Only stir if fries are sticking.
6. Drain fries on the prepared baking sheet, season with salt, and toss. Serve immediately. Eat your fries. Eat them.

Cooking Tips

Check in every few minutes to make sure the fries are at a low simmer, and keep a close eye on them after you turn up the temperature. You want light, golden-brown, and crisp fries, not burnt ones. Serve with Krusty Burgers (see recipe in Chapter 2).

ENJOY OUR PARTY SNACKS PLATTER

 "The War of the Simpsons," Season 2

If you're having a classy house party, you've got to have horse do-vers. Nothing says "ENJOY OUR PARTY SNACKS" like a platter of finger sandwiches that spell out "ENJOY OUR PARTY SNACKS." And if the party goes south, you can always change it to say "BOY OUR PARTY SUCKS."

SERVES 6 AS SANDWICHES OR 12 AS SNACKS

12 large eggs, hard-boiled and peeled
3 tablespoons finely chopped fresh parsley
3 tablespoons minced fresh chives
3 tablespoons mayonnaise
1 tablespoon sour cream or plain yogurt
2 teaspoons brown or Dijon mustard
1 teaspoon fresh lemon juice
Salt and ground black pepper, to taste
Optional: 1 teaspoon milk
12 thin slices soft white sandwich bread

1. Add eggs to a large bowl and mash well with a fork. Add parsley, chives, mayonnaise, sour cream, mustard, and lemon juice and mix. Season with salt and pepper. If egg salad is too thick for your liking, add more mayonnaise or milk.
2. Divide egg salad among 6 bread slices. Spread evenly and top each with another bread slice.
3. Use a sharp knife to trim the crusts from each sandwich. Slice each sandwich into four long rectangles. Cut rectangles into halves or thirds, skewer with toothpicks, and serve on a large platter.

Cooking Tips

An electric pressure cooker is a great tool for making easy-to-peel hard-boiled eggs. Add the steamer rack and enough water so that it reaches just underneath the rack. Add the eggs in a single layer and cook at high pressure for 4 minutes. Let the pressure come down naturally for 5 minutes and then release the pressure. Add the eggs to an ice bath and peel once cooled. To spell out "ENJOY OUR PARTY SNACKS," increase the ingredients in this recipe by 50 percent to make 9 sandwiches. After trimming the crusts, cut each sandwich into four long strips. Cut twelve strips in half and eight strips into thirds. There may pieces leftover.

DRYYYYYY CRACKERS

 "Bart on the Road," Season 7

Crackers, ho! If you've ever wondered how crackers get salted, then wonder no more. This homemade recipe is tasty enough to be the number one cracker in town, besting Table Time and Allied Biscuit.

MAKES 72 CRACKERS

1¼ cups whole-wheat flour
1 cup all-purpose flour
1 teaspoon kosher salt, divided
1 large egg
¼ cup plus 1 teaspoon extra-virgin
  olive oil, divided
¼ cup water
Optional Toppings: Sesame seeds,
  poppy seeds, flaxseeds

1. Combine flours and ½ teaspoon salt in the bowl of a food processor or stand mixer. In a separate small bowl, whisk together egg, ¼ cup oil, and water.
2. With the food processor or stand mixer running, slowly add in egg mixture. Scrape down the sides to incorporate all ingredients. Mix until a soft dough forms, slowly adding more water 1 tablespoon at a time if needed. Dough should be pliant but not sticky. If too wet, add a little more flour.
3. Form dough into a ball and knead a few times to just bring it together. Wrap ball in plastic wrap and let rest at room temperature 15 minutes.
4. Preheat oven to 375°F. Line two large rimmed baking sheets with parchment paper.
5. Divide dough into two equal portions. On a clean surface, roll one portion out into a thin rectangle, rotating after the first few passes to keep it from sticking to the surface. Make dough as thin and even as possible without tearing it—around 16" long. Lift dough and place it on one baking sheet, gently stretching it out flat. Repeat with remaining dough.

Cooking Tips

The thinner these crackers are, the more deliciously crisp they are. But watch them closely while they bake to ensure none of them burn.

6. Brush dough with remaining 1 teaspoon oil. Sprinkle with remaining ½ teaspoon salt and any optional toppings. Lightly press into the top of each sheet of dough with the rolling pin, making it slightly thinner.

7. Use a fork to pierce the "d'oh!" all over. Use a pizza cutter or sharp knife to cut dough sheets into 72 cracker-sized squares.

8. Bake 15 minutes or until lightly golden brown and crisp. If baking both sheets at once, rotate midway through baking. Keep a close eye on sheets, as crackers can go from crisp to burnt quickly. Cool completely on sheets, about 30 minutes, before storing in a large airtight container at room temperature for up to 1 week.

BART'S AMERICA BALLS

 "The Principal and the Pauper," Season 9

Ooh, a fresh batch of Bart's America Balls! Honor Skinner's army days with this patriotic (dog food–free) appetizer.

SERVES 4

For Barbecue Sauce

¾ cup ketchup

¼ cup apple cider vinegar

2 tablespoons packed light brown sugar

2 tablespoons molasses

1 tablespoon water

1 teaspoon spicy brown mustard

1 teaspoon Worcestershire sauce

1 teaspoon smoked paprika

1 teaspoon kosher salt

½ teaspoon ground black pepper

For Meatballs

1 pound 80–85% ground beef or pork (or a mixture)

1 large egg

½ cup plain bread crumbs

1 medium garlic clove, peeled and minced

1 teaspoon kosher salt

1 tablespoon extra-virgin olive oil

1. To make Barbecue Sauce: Combine ketchup, vinegar, brown sugar, molasses, water, mustard, Worcestershire sauce, paprika, salt, and pepper in a medium saucepan. Stir over medium-low heat and bring to a simmer. Reduce heat to low and let simmer, stirring often, 15 minutes while preparing Meatballs.

2. To make Meatballs: Combine beef, egg, bread crumbs, garlic, and salt in a large mixing bowl. Mix with your hands until just combined. Form mixture into 1" balls.

3. Heat a medium skillet over medium heat. Once hot, add oil and coat pan. Add Meatballs. Cook until brown on all sides, about 12 minutes total.

4. Add Meatballs to the pan with Barbecue Sauce. Toss well to coat completely. Simmer meatballs 5 minutes, tossing often.

5. Serve Meatballs on a large platter with little American flags.

Cooking Tips

Instead of panfrying the Meatballs, you can broil them. Use the method outlined in Spaghetti and Moe Balls (see recipe in Chapter 4), checking for doneness after 6 minutes.

NACHO HAT

 "Homer Loves Flanders," Season 5

Do you want to be a nacho man? Then you're going to need a Nacho Hat. If your best friend Flanders isn't around to buy you one, make your own edible hat at home.

SERVES 6

3 cups all-purpose flour, plus extra for dusting

1½ teaspoons table salt

5 tablespoons unsalted butter, cubed, at room temperature

¾ cup warm water

2 tablespoons vegetable oil, divided

1 teaspoon kosher salt

1 (15-ounce) jar cheese dip

1. Add flour and table salt to a large bowl and mix. Add butter and use your hands to mix, squishing butter into flour until mixture resembles cornmeal.
2. Make a well in the middle of the flour mixture and add water and 1½ tablespoons oil. Draw flour mixture into the middle and mix together to form a dough.
3. Knead dough on a clean flat surface 5 minutes until a smooth ball forms. If dough is too shaggy, add more water until it comes together. If dough is too sticky, add more flour.
4. Rub dough ball with ½ teaspoon oil and place it back in the bowl. Cover and let rest at least 30 minutes, up to 1 hour.
5. Line a 6" round cake pan inside and out with aluminum foil. Line the inside of a 10" round cake pan with aluminum foil (an 8" round cake pan and 12" round cake pan also work). Set the smaller pan in the middle of the larger pan, opening side up. Use several large pieces of aluminum foil to line the entire set inside and along the inner edges.

6. Preheat oven to 375°F. Lightly flour a clean flat surface and roll dough out evenly into a large circle about ¼" thick.
7. Center dough over the lined pans and gently lay it on top. Starting in the middle, press dough into the mold, being careful not to tear dough or stretch it too thin.
8. Trim excess dough and smooth out the edge. Brush with remaining 1 teaspoon oil and sprinkle with kosher salt. Place on a large baking sheet.
9. Bake 35 minutes or until top edges are golden brown and recesses are cooked through. If any bubbles pop up during baking, gently poke with a fork and press back down. Let cool completely in mold, at least 30 minutes.
10. Turn oven up to 400°F. Remove cooled hat from mold and flip it over on the baking sheet. Bake about 10 minutes, watching carefully to make sure it doesn't brown too much. Let cool on sheet, about 30 minutes.
11. Heat up cheese dip in the microwave until warm. Add to "bowl" of Nacho Hat.

OFFICIAL
PRETZEL
INSPECTOR

MARGE'S PRETZELS

 "The Twisted World of Marge Simpson," Season 8

Whether you're starting your own pretzel wagon or just want something to throw onto the baseball field, these soft pretzels will do the trick.

MAKES 8 PRETZELS

¾ cup warm water, divided
2 teaspoons granulated sugar
2 teaspoons kosher salt, divided
1 (¼-ounce) packet active dry yeast
3 cups all-purpose flour, plus extra for dusting
2 tablespoons melted butter
1 cup boiling water
2 tablespoons baking soda
1 large egg yolk
1 tablespoon room-temperature water

1. Stir together ½ cup warm water, sugar, and 1 teaspoon salt in a large mixing bowl or the bowl of a stand mixer. Sprinkle yeast over the top and let sit 5 minutes.
2. Add flour and melted butter and mix with a wooden spoon or the paddle attachment of the stand mixer. Add more warm water, 2 tablespoons at a time, and mix until a soft, pliant dough forms.
3. Knead dough with your hands or the dough hook of the stand mixer 7 minutes or until soft and smooth. If dough is too dry, sprinkle with water. If too sticky, sprinkle with flour. Once smooth, place in a large, lightly oiled bowl, cover, and let rise at room temperature about 45 minutes or until doubled in size.
4. Preheat oven to 450°F. Line two large baking sheets with parchment paper and lightly grease.
5. Transfer dough to a clean work surface sprayed lightly with nonstick cooking oil and divide into 8 equal pieces. Allow pieces to rest 5 minutes.

(continued ▶ *)*

6. While dough rests, combine boiling water and baking soda in a shallow bowl, stirring until soda is mostly dissolved.

7. Roll a piece of dough into a long, thin rope as close to 30" long as possible. Arrange into a U shape and cross the two ends in the middle, twisting together once. Press the ends into the curve of the U to form a pretzel shape.

8. Place pretzel in baking soda solution, spooning it over the top of the dough to completely coat it. Lift, let drain, and place on prepared baking sheet. Repeat with remaining dough.

9. Allow pretzels to rest 10 minutes. While resting, beat egg yolk in a small bowl with room temperature water. Brush pretzels with egg wash and sprinkle with remaining 1 teaspoon salt.

10. Bake pretzels about 13 minutes or until they are a deep golden brown, rotating pans midway through baking. Eat warm or throw at Whitey Ford.

WEDDING RING ONION RINGS

 "I Married Marge," Season 3

If you can't afford a decent wedding ring, then crispy onion rings are the next best thing. They come in different sizes sure to fit any finger—just don't put them on while they're hot.

SERVES 2

1 large sweet onion, peeled, sliced into rings, and separated
1 quart canola oil
½ cup all-purpose flour
¼ cup cornstarch
¾ teaspoon baking powder
½ cup light beer or soda water
Salt, to taste

1. Place onion rings in a large bowl and cover with boiling water. Let sit 15 minutes, then drain and dry rings well with a tea towel or paper towels.
2. Add 2" canola oil to a large Dutch oven or heavy-bottomed pan. Heat over medium-high heat to 375°F.
3. When oil has almost reached temperature, combine flour, cornstarch, and baking powder in a medium bowl. Add beer while whisking with a fork. Add more beer as needed until batter is thick enough to stick to onion rings but thin enough to coat them.
4. Add ½ of the onion rings to batter and gently toss to coat.
5. Once oil is ready, use a fork to lift an onion ring and let the excess batter drip off. Add ring to oil and fry 4 minutes. Repeat battering and frying with remaining rings, careful not to overlap in frying pot. Onion rings are done when crispy and golden brown.
6. Transfer rings to a large paper towel–lined baking sheet to drain and immediately sprinkle with salt. Serve warm.

CHAPTER 4

DINNER

Sometimes Slender Vittles frozen dinners just won't cut it. And sometimes it's fun to dress up for dinner and use the good china. So gather the family around the dinner table for Marge's Pork Chops served alongside mashed potatoes that can easily be sculpted into a circus tent. Or claim your rightful place

as the Pope of Chilitown with Chief Wiggum's Chili, packed with spicy roasted peppers (they taste like burning). If you can't stand to cook your delicious friend Pinchy, then one of the dinner recipes in this chapter is sure to ease your hunger pangs.

LITTLE MEATLOAF MEN

 "Mr. Lisa Goes to Washington," Season 3

Wow, Little Meatloaf Men! Put down that magazine for a minute and make a fun and flavorful dinner the whole family will love. They're really, really, really...good.

SERVES 4

2 teaspoons extra-virgin olive oil

½ medium yellow onion, peeled and finely diced

½ medium green bell pepper, seeded and finely diced, plus 1 tablespoon small slices for decorating

1 large garlic clove, peeled and minced

1 heaping cup finely diced button mushrooms

1 large egg

2 tablespoons ketchup

2 teaspoons spicy brown mustard

1 teaspoon Worcestershire sauce

1 pound lean ground beef

½ cup panko bread crumbs

¼ cup finely grated Parmesan cheese

1 teaspoon kosher salt

½ teaspoon ground black pepper

1 tablespoon jarred diced pimentos or finely diced red bell pepper

1. Preheat oven to 350°F and line a large rimmed baking sheet with parchment paper or aluminum foil.

2. Heat a medium skillet over medium heat and add oil. Add onion and cook 3 minutes, stirring occasionally. Add diced bell pepper and garlic and cook 3 more minutes.

3. Add mushrooms and cook 4 minutes more or until vegetables are cooked through and onion is translucent. Remove skillet from heat and set aside.

4. In a large bowl, whisk together egg, ketchup, mustard, and Worcestershire sauce.

5. Add beef, bread crumbs, Parmesan, salt, black pepper, and cooked vegetables to egg mixture. Mix until well combined.

6. Lightly spray inside and outside of a gingerbread man cookie cutter with nonstick cooking spray. Place cutter on the prepared baking sheet. Use a spoon or your hands to fill cutter with some meatloaf mixture. Pack meatloaf tightly.

(continued ▶ *)*

Cooking Tips

Be sure to chop the vegetables small—it'll help your meatloaf
men keep their shapes.

7. To remove the cookie cutter, use one hand to lightly
   press mixture down while carefully lifting the cutter
   up with your other hand. Repeat with remaining
   meatloaf mixture.
8. Bake about 25 minutes, depending on the size of
   your cookie cutter, until Little Meatloaf Men are
   browned and cooked through and register 160°F
   internally.
9. Let cool 5 minutes on baking sheet.
10. Transfer to a large serving platter. Use remaining
    sliced green bell pepper and pimentos to create
    mouths and eyes. Serve.

PAUL AND LINDA MCCARTNEY'S LENTIL SOUP

 "Lisa the Vegetarian," Season 7

Did you know that if you play "Maybe I'm Amazed" backward, you'll hear a recipe for a really ripping lentil soup? It's hearty and delicious, perfect for sharing with your vegetarian (and vegan) friends in a garden in the shade.

SERVES 2

2 tablespoons vegetable oil
1 medium yellow onion, peeled and chopped
1 cup chopped carrots
2 medium ribs celery, chopped
1 medium garlic clove, peeled and crushed
1 tablespoon chopped fresh parsley
Salt and ground black pepper, to taste
½ cup green or brown lentils, picked over, rinsed, and drained
2¼ cups vegetable broth or water
1 bay leaf

1. Heat a medium saucepan over medium heat and add oil. Add onion, carrots, and celery and stir. Cook, stirring occasionally, until onion is mostly translucent, about 5 minutes.
2. Add garlic and parsley and stir. Cook 1 more minute until fragrant. Season with salt and pepper.
3. Add lentils, broth, and bay leaf. Bring to a boil over high heat.
4. Reduce heat to low, cover, and simmer until lentils are tender, about 45 minutes.
5. Remove bay leaf and season again to taste. Serve hot in medium bowls.

Cooking Tips

This recipe is easy to double or even triple, and it makes great leftovers.

Recipe Variations

Try these additions for more flavor: Double or triple the garlic. Add 1–2 cups chopped mushrooms and/or smoked paprika with the garlic and parsley. Add 2 tablespoons white or red wine after adding the garlic and simmer for a couple of minutes before adding the lentils. Add 2 teaspoons tomato paste and/or up to 2 cups fresh spinach in the last few minutes of cooking. Finish the soup with more fresh parsley and a squeeze of lemon juice or a drizzle of red wine vinegar.

TACO PLATTER

 "Krusty Gets Busted," Season 1

Anyone who has to sit through one of Patty and Selma's slideshows deserves a Taco Platter. While this recipe isn't a true "Mexican delicacy," it *is* a crowd-pleaser. Homemade taco seasoning makes it better than your average hard-shell taco night.

SERVES 4

1 pound lean ground beef
2 teaspoons chili powder
½ teaspoon ground cumin
½ teaspoon smoked or sweet paprika
¼ teaspoon garlic powder
¼ teaspoon dried oregano
⅛ teaspoon cayenne pepper
Salt and ground black pepper, to taste
2 tablespoons water
12 hard taco shells
Optional Toppings: Shredded Cheddar or jack cheese, shredded lettuce, diced tomatoes, taco sauce or hot sauce

1. Add beef to a large nonstick skillet over medium heat. Cook, breaking up chunks, until no pink remains, about 5 minutes. Drain fat. Return pan to heat.
2. Add chili powder, cumin, paprika, garlic powder, oregano, and cayenne, and season with salt and black pepper. Add water and stir until beef is well coated. Reduce the heat to low. If beef starts to get dry, sprinkle with more water and toss.
3. Heat taco shells in oven or microwave according to the package directions.
4. Fill each taco shell with seasoned beef. Top with cheese, lettuce, tomatoes, and sauce (if using). Serve immediately on a platter.

Cooking Tips

If you're vegetarian, swap the ground beef with your favorite meat substitute. You may want to use less water and not drain the fat, as veggie "meats" tend to have more water and less oil than beef.

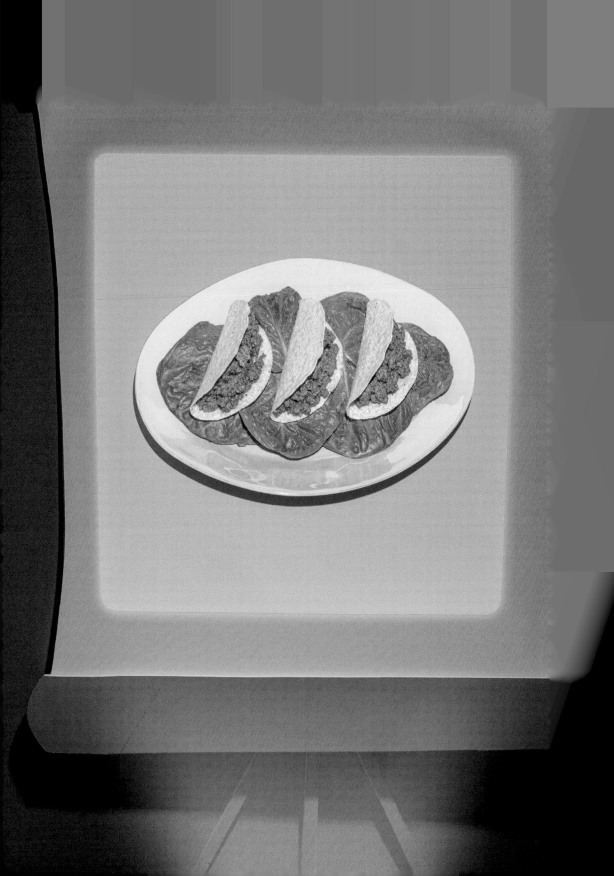

SKINNER'S VIETNAMESE STEW

 "Team Homer," Season 7

One taste of this coconut curry and you'll understand why it pushed Skinner close to madness. With fish, vegetables, prawns, and four kinds of rice, it's quality prison food. Use Madras curry powder to get the spices just right.

SERVES 4

2 medium stalks lemongrass, trimmed and roughly chopped

1 (1") knob ginger, peeled and chopped

1 small yellow onion, peeled and roughly chopped

1 large garlic clove, peeled

2 tablespoons Madras curry powder

¼ teaspoon salt, plus more to taste

¼ cup water

2 tablespoons vegetable oil

4 large carrots, peeled and cut into ½" chunks

1 cup full-fat coconut milk

1 cup chicken broth or water

6 stalks baby bok choy, ends trimmed and leaves separated

1 tablespoon fish sauce

1 pound tilapia fillets, cut into 1" chunks

1 pound tail-on shrimp, peeled and deveined

2 large limes, 1 halved and 1 cut into wedges

4 cups cooked Thai wild rice blend

Optional: Fresh cilantro, for garnish

1. Add lemongrass and ginger to a food processor or blender. Pulse five times to chop. Add onion, garlic, curry powder, and salt. Process until a fragrant yellow paste forms, adding up to ¼ cup water and scraping down sides as needed.

2. Heat oil over medium heat in a heavy-bottomed pot. Add lemongrass paste and cook, stirring, 3 minutes. Add carrots and stir.

3. Add coconut milk and broth and turn heat up to medium-high. Once simmering, lower heat to medium-low and simmer 10 minutes.

4. Add bok choy and fish sauce and stir. Cover and simmer 3 minutes or until greens are just wilted. Add water if sauce becomes too dry.

5. Season tilapia and shrimp with salt to taste and add to curry. Stir and cook until opaque and cooked through, about 3 minutes.

6. Remove pot from heat and let sit 5 minutes. Add juice of ½ lime, taste, and add more lime juice or salt as desired. Serve on large plates with rice and garnish with lime wedges and cilantro (if using).

Recipe Variations

Any type of firm white fish will work well in this recipe. If you don't have a Thai rice blend, use white or brown rice and cook according to the package directions.

YOU DON'T MAKE FRIENDS WITH SALAD

 "Lisa the Vegetarian," Season 7

While others might mock you with a conga line, you could actually make some friends with this flavorful salad. Featuring one of Lisa's favorite vegetables (beets!), it'll please carnivores and vegetarians alike.

SERVES 4

3 medium (or 4 small) beets, trimmed

¼ cup plus 1 teaspoon extra-virgin olive oil, divided

¼ cup freshly squeezed orange juice

2 teaspoons apple cider vinegar

1 teaspoon honey

Salt and ground black pepper, to taste

4 cups packed fresh arugula or baby spinach

1 large avocado, peeled, pitted, and diced

⅓ cup crumbled feta cheese

3 tablespoons shelled roasted pistachios

1. Preheat oven to 425°F. Coat beets in 1 teaspoon oil and wrap tightly in aluminum foil. Place on a large ungreased baking sheet.
2. Roast beets 40 minutes or until easily pierced with a knife. Carefully unwrap foil and let beets cool about 10 minutes.
3. Whisk together remaining ¼ cup oil, orange juice, vinegar, and honey. Season with salt and pepper.
4. Add arugula to a large bowl. Toss with dressing.
5. Peel and chop cooled beets. Add to salad along with avocado, feta, and pistachios. Serve.

Recipe Variations

Swap the pistachios for toasted walnuts. Toss in a segmented orange or two for a burst of citrus.

MARGE'S PORK CHOPS

 "Itchy & Scratchy & Marge," Season 2

Even though she insists they're nothing special, Marge makes the best pork chops. Bonus: They can be eaten on the Bigfoot Diet.

SERVES 4

1 teaspoon kosher salt
½ teaspoon ground black pepper
½ teaspoon dried rosemary, crushed
1 smidgen (½ teaspoon) dried thyme
½ teaspoon turmeric
¼ teaspoon dried marjoram
1 sprinkle (¼ teaspoon) dried chervil or parsley
1 whisper (⅛ teaspoon) MSG
4 (8-ounce) bone-in pork chops
1 tablespoon extra-virgin olive oil

1. Preheat oven to 375°F. Heat a large ovenproof skillet over medium-high heat.
2. Combine salt, pepper, rosemary, thyme, turmeric, marjoram, chervil, and MSG in a small bowl. Rub into pork chops on both sides.
3. Once skillet is hot, add oil to coat the bottom. Add pork chops in a single layer and cook 4 minutes or until bottoms are browned. Flip chops and transfer skillet to oven.
4. Bake 10 minutes or until thickest part of chops registers at 145°F internally. Let chops rest 5 minutes in pan before serving.

Cooking Tips

If you have huge pork chops approaching 1 pound each, double the spices. Baking may take as long as 20 minutes if they are very thick.

Recipe Variations

This recipe uses Marge's exact blend of spices (plus some salt and pepper), but you can mix things up to suit your preferences. Some tasty options include garlic powder, onion powder, paprika, red pepper flakes, and oregano. Or swap all of the spices for a tasty premade spice blend.

SPAGHETTI AND MOE BALLS

 "Bart Sells His Soul," Season 7

It's hard to pick a dish at Uncle Moe's Family Feedbag. Between the Southwestern Pizza Fingers and the Guilt-Free Steak-Fish Fillets, it's all awesomely outrageous. If you're not too busy getting your soul back, this classic Spaghetti and Moe Balls is sure to please.

SERVES 4

10 ounces uncooked spaghetti

1 teaspoon extra-virgin olive oil

2 medium garlic cloves, peeled and minced, divided

1 (28-ounce) can whole plum tomatoes

1 teaspoon kosher salt, plus more to taste

1 pound ground meat (beef, pork, lamb, turkey, chicken, or a combination)

1 large egg

½ cup plain bread crumbs

2 tablespoons finely grated Parmesan cheese, plus more for garnish

2 teaspoons minced fresh parsley or basil

1 pinch (1/16 teaspoon) red pepper flakes

1. Bring a large pot of salted water to a boil over high heat. Once boiling, add spaghetti. Stir and cook according to the package directions until al dente. Drain, cover, and set aside.

2. Heat oil in a separate medium saucepan over medium heat. Add 1 minced garlic clove and cook 30 seconds, until fragrant. Add tomatoes and juice, breaking them up with your hands as you add them. Season to taste with salt and allow to simmer while you make meatballs, stirring occasionally.

3. In a large mixing bowl, combine ground meat, egg, bread crumbs, Parmesan, parsley, red pepper flakes, 1 teaspoon salt, and remaining 1 minced garlic clove. Mix with your hands until just combined. Roll into 1¼" balls. You should have roughly 16 meatballs.

4. Preheat broiler to high. Lightly grease a large rimmed baking sheet with oil and transfer meatballs to sheet. Broil until browned and firm, about 8 minutes, turning once halfway through broiling.

5. Add broiled meatballs to tomato sauce and let simmer over low heat until ready to serve.

6. Divide pasta evenly among four plates or bowls. Top with sauce, Moe Balls, and more Parmesan to taste. Serve and *smile*!

Cooking Tips

For extra-flavorful meatballs, swap half of the meat for sweet or spicy Italian sausage.

If you'd like a smoother sauce, blend the tomatoes before adding them to the pan. A jarred tomato sauce will also work in a pinch.

If you only eat food in bar form, compress your serving into a spaghetti bar.

CHIEF WIGGUM'S CHILI

 "El Viaje Misterioso de Nuestro Jomer," Season 8

You may have trouble finding the merciless peppers of Quetzlzacatenango at the grocery store, so use whatever hot peppers are available. But beware! Even without the insanity peppers, the heat might send you on a spiritual journey.

SERVES 4

1 large poblano pepper, halved lengthwise and seeded

2 medium jalapeño peppers, halved lengthwise and seeded

12 assorted small hot peppers (like habanero and serrano), whole

1 tablespoon vegetable oil, divided

1 small yellow onion, peeled and diced

1 pound lean ground beef

½ medium bell pepper, seeded and diced

2 medium garlic cloves, peeled and minced

1 heaping tablespoon chili powder

1 teaspoon ground cumin

Salt and ground black pepper, to taste

1 (8-ounce) can tomato sauce

1 (15-ounce) can pinto beans, rinsed and drained

1 (15-ounce) can kidney beans, rinsed and drained

1. Preheat the broiler to high. Rub poblano, jalapeño, and hot peppers with 1 teaspoon oil and place on a large ungreased baking sheet.
2. Broil peppers, flipping halfway through, until charred on both sides, about 6 minutes. Set aside whole hot peppers and dice poblano and jalapeños.
3. Add remaining 2 teaspoons oil to a large heavy pot and heat over medium heat. Once hot, add onion and stir. Cook about 3 minutes, until onion begins to turn translucent.
4. Add beef, bell pepper, and garlic to the pot. Break up meat and stir until cooked through, about 5 minutes. If desired, drain off some fat once cooked. Add poblano and jalapeños, chili powder, cumin, salt, and black pepper. Cook 1 more minute, stirring.

Recipe Variations

This chili is also delicious with ground turkey or vegetarian "meat." Or leave out the beef altogether and replace it with a third can of beans.

Cooking Tips

Leave the whole peppers out for a mildly spicy chili that won't totally kick your butt. For a truly mild chili, omit the jalapeños. To add some serious heat, chop the broiled hot peppers before adding them to the chili. If possible, wear gloves while handling hot peppers, including jalapeños, and crack a window to avoid extra irritation.

5. Add tomato sauce. Fill empty sauce can with water and add to pot. Stir and bring to a simmer. Cover and reduce heat to low, simmering 30 minutes.

6. Stir and add in beans and charred whole hot peppers, covering and cooking another 10 minutes. Add water if chili becomes too dry, and more salt and black pepper to taste.

7. Serve in medium bowls with several mugs of beer and a lit candle.

CIRCUS TENT MASHED POTATOES

 "Homie the Clown," Season 6

If you find yourself compulsively sculpting these mashed potatoes into a circus tent, then don't let your family stand in the way. Go to clown college!

SERVES 6

3 pounds potatoes (mix of russets and Yukon Gold), peeled and cut into 1" cubes
¼ cup (½ stick) butter, cubed
¼ cup sour cream
Salt and ground black pepper, to taste

1. Place potatoes in a large pot and add enough water to cover by 1". Bring to a boil over high heat and cook about 15 minutes or until potatoes are very tender.
2. Drain potatoes over another large pot or heatproof mixing bowl, reserving liquid. Return potatoes to first pot. Mash well. Add ¼ cup cooking liquid and stir. If you're planning to make a circus tent, stop here and let potatoes sit until cool enough to handle, about 20 minutes.
3. To form circus tent, add a big mound of cooled mashed potatoes to a large plate. Build mound up, compacting as you go and forming it into a tentlike shape. Once the general shape has been formed, use wet hands to smooth the outside and add details.
4. For hot, unshaped mashed potatoes, add butter, sour cream, salt, and pepper after mashing. Stir to melt and combine. Add more cooking liquid a couple tablespoons at a time until desired consistency is reached. Serve.

Recipe Variations

Peel a head of roasted garlic and add it to the potatoes before mashing. Swap the sour cream for plain yogurt.

BABY GUTS

 "Itchy & Scratchy Land," Season 6

It's hard to choose when a menu includes Brain Burgers (with extra pus) and Eyeball Stew, but Tavern on the Scream's Baby Guts (veal scallopine) is superb.

SERVES 4

1 pound uncooked spaghetti

2 pints cherry tomatoes

1/2 cup plus 1 tablespoon extra-virgin olive oil, divided

Salt and ground black pepper, to taste

1/3 cup all-purpose flour

1 pound veal cutlets, pounded thin if more than 1/4" thick

4 medium garlic cloves, peeled and minced

1/2 cup dry white wine

1 large lemon, zested and juiced

1/2 cup finely grated Parmesan cheese

1/4 cup chopped fresh parsley

1/4 teaspoon red pepper flakes

1. Bring a large pot of salted water to a boil over high heat. Add spaghetti to boiling water and cook according to package instructions. Before draining, reserve 1 cup pasta cooking water. Transfer pasta to a large bowl, cover, and set aside.

2. Preheat broiler to high. Toss cherry tomatoes in 1 tablespoon oil in a medium bowl, then spread them out on a large ungreased rimmed baking sheet. Season with salt and pepper. Broil about 7 minutes, tossing once or twice, until tomatoes are burst but not burnt.

3. Add flour to a medium shallow bowl or pie plate. Season with salt and pepper.

4. Add 1/4 cup oil to a large skillet and heat over medium-high heat. Salt veal cutlets and then dredge each in flour mixture, making sure to completely cover, and shake off excess.

5. Fry cutlets in a single layer about 2 minutes or until browned. Turn and cook another 2 minutes or so to brown other side and finish cooking (internal temperature should be at least 160°F for medium). Remove to a large paper towel–lined plate and repeat with remaining cutlets.

6. Add remaining ¼ cup oil to the empty, dry pot used for pasta over medium heat. Add garlic and cook about 2 minutes, being careful to not let garlic burn. Add white wine and cook about 3 minutes or until alcohol smell dissipates. Add ⅓ of the reserved pasta water and simmer about 3 minutes more. Turn off heat.

7. Add pasta back to the pot, followed by lemon juice and zest, Parmesan, parsley, and red pepper flakes. Season with salt and black pepper and toss well, adding more pasta water a little at a time to loosen up sauce as needed.

8. To serve, divide pasta among four large plates. Top with tomatoes and cutlets.

Recipe Variations

Swap the cutlets out for chicken breast cutlets if preferred. Pound to $1/4$" thickness before preparing.

MARGE'S OVERGLAZED HAM

 "A Milhouse Divided," Season 8

If you've got a few hours before the dinner party starts, add another coat of glaze to the ham until it's positively glowing.

SERVES 15

1 (10-pound) bone-in cooked ham
1½ cups packed light or dark brown sugar
½ cup honey
1 tablespoon apple cider vinegar
1 tablespoon Dijon or spicy brown mustard
⅛ teaspoon ground cloves
⅛ teaspoon ground nutmeg

1. Let ham sit at room temperature 1 hour. Preheat oven to 325°F. Place a rack inside a large roasting pan and add ¼" water to the pan.
2. Use a knife to score top of ham in a diamond pattern about ¼" deep. Place ham on the rack flat side down and cover with aluminum foil.
3. Bake about 12 minutes per pound or until internal temperature reaches 130°F (around 1–2 hours).
4. Combine brown sugar, honey, vinegar, mustard, cloves, and nutmeg in a medium bowl.
5. Remove ham from oven and turn temperature up to 375°F. Uncover ham and brush with ⅓ of the brown sugar glaze.
6. Return pan to oven and bake ham, uncovered, 10 minutes. Brush with another ⅓ of the glaze and bake another 10 minutes. Repeat with remaining glaze and bake until shiny and internal temperature reaches at least 140°F, about 10–15 minutes.
7. Let ham cool 5 minutes on a cutting board before slicing and serving.

Cooking Tips

A smoked or baked ham will work for this recipe. If using a spiral-cut ham, skip scoring it in a diamond pattern.

THANKSGIVING LEFTOVER SANDWICHES

 "Bart vs. Thanksgiving," Season 2

Holidays with the family can be stressful. But even if your big meal started with the centerpiece burning in the fireplace, try taking one more crack at togetherness by enjoying these Thanksgiving Leftover Sandwiches.

SERVES 4

10 ounces leftover green beans or Brussels sprouts
½ cup leftover gravy
½ cup leftover cranberry sauce
4 leftover rolls or small hoagie rolls
1¼ pounds leftover sliced or shredded turkey

1. Add green beans to a small skillet and reheat over medium heat until warm, about 5 minutes.
2. Microwave gravy in 30-second increments, or heat in a small saucepan over medium-low heat about 5 minutes, until warm.
3. Spread 1 tablespoon cranberry sauce on the bottom half of a roll and 1 tablespoon on the top half. Add to the bottom roll ¼ of the turkey followed by ¼ of the green beans. Drizzle with 2 tablespoons gravy and cover with the top half of the roll. Repeat to make 4 sandwiches total.

Cooking Tips

For a quick cranberry sauce, combine 1 cup fresh or frozen cranberries, ⅓ cup sugar, and ¼ cup orange juice in a small saucepan. Heat over medium heat and stir until boiling. Cook until the cranberries have just popped, about 5 minutes. Let cool and chill in the refrigerator until sandwich time. For a quick gravy, add 2 tablespoons butter and 1 heaping tablespoon minced onion to a small saucepan. Cook over medium heat for 5–10 minutes until onion begins to brown. Add 2 tablespoons flour and stir, cooking 1 minute. Add 1 cup warmed chicken broth and whisk. Bring to a simmer and cook about 5 minutes, until thickened. Season and serve.

CHAPTER 5

DESSERT

Make sure everyone gets their just desserts with the sweet recipes in this chapter. Including all of the major food groups—fats and sweets, empty calories, chocotastic, whipped, and congealed—you'll find a dish for every occasion. Far superior to a bowl of wintergreen nonfat ice milk, A Big Pile of Brownies or a batch of Caramel Cods is celebration-worthy. If your loved one is known to devour entire desserts in the blink of an eye (like Homer), then make a whole cake for them to ruin. Some desserts can even be used for trapping and science experiments—results not guaranteed.

LISA'S CHOCOLATE-CHERRY EXPERIMENT CUPCAKES

 "Duffless," Season 4

Cupcakes, cupcakes! Sweet cakes for all! Whether you're looking to torture your brother or simply end your meal on a sweet note, these chocolate and cherry cupcakes are worth a few zaps.

MAKES 12 CUPCAKES

For Cupcakes

1 cup all-purpose flour
1 cup granulated sugar
1/2 cup cocoa powder
1 teaspoon baking powder
1/2 teaspoon baking soda
1/2 teaspoon salt
1/2 cup whole milk
1/4 cup canola oil
1 large egg, beaten
1 1/2 teaspoons vanilla extract
1/2 cup hot coffee
12 maraschino cherries, stemmed, drained

For Frosting

1 (7-ounce) container marshmallow creme
1/2 cup (1 stick) unsalted butter, at room temperature
1/2 cup powdered sugar, plus more for thickening
1/2 teaspoon almond extract
1/8 teaspoon salt
12 maraschino cherries with stems, drained

1. Preheat oven to 325°F. Line a twelve-cup muffin pan with cupcake liners and spray lightly with nonstick cooking spray.
2. To make Cupcakes: Whisk together flour, sugar, cocoa powder, baking powder, baking soda, and salt in a large bowl.
3. Add milk, oil, egg, and vanilla. Mix until combined. Slowly add hot coffee while mixing. Beat batter 1 minute, scraping sides. Batter will be runny.
4. Fill prepared liners slightly over halfway. Add 1 cherry to the middle of each Cupcake. (Lay them on top; they will sink while baking.)
5. Bake Cupcakes 20 minutes or until a toothpick inserted comes out clean. Remove Cupcakes from pan and let cool completely, about 1 hour.
6. To make Frosting: Add marshmallow creme, butter, powdered sugar, almond extract, and salt to a medium mixing bowl. Beat about 3 minutes until completely combined and creamy. For a stiffer mixture, add more powdered sugar.
7. Decorate Cupcakes with Frosting and top each with a cherry.

Cooking Tips

Serve up frosted Cupcakes immediately or store in a container in the refrigerator for up to 1 day. Unfrosted Cupcakes will keep for up to 3 days.

DELICIOUS GELATIN DESSERT

 "There's No Disgrace Like Home," Season 1

Score points with the boss by mixing up some colorful, slimy goop for your next work event or potluck. If green isn't your color, don't worry—there's a whole rainbow of possibilities.

SERVES 6

1 (3-ounce) package lime-flavored gelatin dessert mix
1 cup boiling water
¾ cup pineapple juice, chilled
¼ cup drained, squeezed dry, and chilled packed crushed pineapple
½ cup mini marshmallows

1. Grease a gelatin mold lightly with nonstick cooking spray.
2. In a medium mixing bowl, combine gelatin mix and boiling water and stir about 3 minutes, until completely dissolved.
3. Add chilled pineapple juice and stir. Set bowl over a larger bowl filled halfway with ice and cold water, creating an ice water bath. Let sit, stirring occasionally, until mixture has started to set up into a loose gel that wobbles slightly, about 35 minutes. Check consistency often: It needs to be thick enough to suspend the fruit and marshmallows throughout but shouldn't be so solid that you can't easily add remaining ingredients.

(continued ▶ *)*

Cooking Tips

Use a chilled 20-ounce can crushed pineapple in juice for both the fruit and the juice in this recipe. And check out your mold before starting. To measure the size of your mold, fill it with water and then measure the water. This recipe makes about 2½ cups of mixture, making it perfect for a mold that holds 3–4 cups. If you're using an extra-large mold, double the recipe and allow more time for it to set.

Recipe Variations

Make a red gelatin dessert by swapping the lime gelatin for cherry and replacing the pineapple with fresh raspberries. Make an orange version by using orange gelatin, swapping the pineapple juice for orange juice, and replacing the pineapple with drained mandarin orange segments. For a yellow gelatin dessert, use lemon or pineapple gelatin and swap the crushed pineapple for drained fruit cocktail.

4. Fold in crushed pineapple and marshmallows and add mixture to prepared mold, tapping it on a counter to expel any bubbles.
5. Chill uncovered in the refrigerator at least 3 hours until completely set.
6. Place a large plate upside down over the top of the mold, then quickly flip it over, leaving the inverted mold on top of the plate. Let sit a few moments to let gelatin slide out of the mold. If gelatin doesn't move, dip mold (without getting gelatin wet) in warm water for a few seconds and try again.
7. Serve immediately or refrigerate, covered, until serving (for up to 3 days).

MARTIN'S RAISIN ROUNDIES

 "Sweet Seymour Skinner's Baadasssss Song," Season 5

Need to suck up to your teacher? You can't go wrong with chewy, sweet, and lightly spiced oatmeal raisin cookies. Santa's Little Helper gives them two paws up.

MAKES ABOUT 30 COOKIES

¾ cup all-purpose flour
1 teaspoon ground cinnamon
½ teaspoon baking soda
¼ teaspoon salt
½ cup (1 stick) unsalted butter, at room temperature
½ cup packed light brown sugar
1 large egg
1 teaspoon vanilla extract
1½ cups rolled oats
1 cup raisins

1. Whisk together flour, cinnamon, baking soda, and salt in a small mixing bowl. Set aside.
2. Add butter and brown sugar to a medium mixing bowl. Cream together with a hand mixer about 1 minute, until fluffy and pale. Add egg and vanilla and beat until well mixed and smooth.
3. Add flour mixture to butter mixture and mix until just combined. Stir in oats and raisins. Cover bowl and chill dough at least 20 minutes or up to 1 hour.
4. Preheat oven to 350°F. Line two large baking sheets with parchment paper or silicone mats.
5. Using a cookie scoop or spoon, form the dough into 30 (1") balls and place 2" apart on prepared sheets.
6. Bake cookies 11–12 minutes. If baking sheets are on different racks in the oven, swap them midbake. When done, cookies will be light brown around the edges but still shiny in the middle.
7. Cool 3 minutes on baking sheets before transferring to a cooling rack. The cookies will keep up to 4 days in an airtight container at room temperature. Keep away from cute dogs.

Recipe Variations

Swap half of the raisins for chocolate chips for extra sweetness, or chopped nuts for a bit of crunch.

SPECIAL CAKE FOR HOMER TO RUIN

 "Lady Bouvier's Lover," Season 5

Hey hey hey! Stop ruining your kid's birthday cake and eat this special cake instead! Decorated with random letters, it tastes better than it looks.

SERVES 8

For Cake

1 (15¼-ounce) box white cake mix
3 large egg whites
1 cup water
⅓ cup vegetable oil
⅓ cup cocoa powder, sifted
2 tablespoons brewed coffee, at room temperature

For Frosting

8 ounces cream cheese, at room temperature
½ cup (1 stick) unsalted butter, at room temperature
1 teaspoon vanilla extract
¼ teaspoon salt
2½ cups powdered sugar, sifted
Optional: ½ cup mini chocolate chips
1 (1-pound) package multicolored fondant

1. To make Cake: Preheat oven and prepare two 8" or 9" cake pans according to cake mix instructions.
2. In a large bowl, combine cake mix, egg whites, water, and oil.
3. Scoop 1¾ cups batter into a separate large bowl. Add cocoa powder and coffee and mix until well combined.
4. Add ¼ cup chocolate batter to the center of each prepared pan. Top with ¼ cup plain batter (this will push chocolate batter outward). Repeat with remaining batter, alternating adding ¼ cup each flavor to the center of the prepared pans.
5. Bake according to cake mix instructions. Once baked, let cakes cool in pans 5 minutes before turning out onto cooling racks and letting cool completely, about 1 hour.

(continued ▶)

Recipe Variations

You can easily make this a "HAPPY BIRTHDAY MAGAGGIE" cake. Keep all the cake mix white, leaving out the cocoa powder and coffee, and bake as directed. Use pink food coloring to tint the frosting pink, and generously frost the cakes between the layers and on top, letting some frosting hang off the sides. Add a "1" candle and letters to spell "HAPPY BIRTHDAY MAGAGGIE."

6. To make Frosting: Add cream cheese, butter, vanilla, and salt to a medium mixing bowl. Beat until creamy and fluffy. Add powdered sugar. Beat on low until incorporated, then on high until fluffy and well mixed.

7. Place one cooled cake layer on a large plate or cake stand. Add slightly less than $\frac{1}{3}$ of the frosting to the top and spread evenly. Top with mini chocolate chips (if using). Place second cake layer on top. Use remaining frosting to cover top and sides, creating a smooth surface. Chill while you make the decorations.

8. Roll out portions of colored fondant according to package directions. Use letter cutters or trace paper cutouts to cut an assortment of letters. Place letters all over cake. Set aside for Homer to ruin.

LA BOMBE ÉCLAIRS

 "Guess Who's Coming to Criticize Dinner?," Season 11

While these giant éclairs aren't over a million calories and full of poison, they are deadly delicious.

MAKES 8 GIANT ÉCLAIRS

1 cup water
½ cup (1 stick) unsalted butter
¼ teaspoon salt
1¼ cups all-purpose flour
4 large eggs
1 cup heavy whipping cream, divided
1½ cups prepared vanilla pudding
½ cup dark or semisweet chocolate chips

1. Preheat oven to 425°F. Line a large baking sheet with parchment paper.
2. Combine water, butter, and salt in a medium saucepan. Heat over medium heat until butter is melted and mixture is rapidly boiling.
3. Once boiling, remove mixture from heat and add flour, mixing vigorously with a wooden spoon. Return to heat and stir about 1 minute or until mixture is well mixed and follows the spoon around the pan.
4. Remove from heat and let cool to 125°F or just cool enough that you can poke your finger in mixture and leave it for a few seconds (about 3–10 minutes, depending on kitchen temperature).
5. Add eggs 1 at a time, beating after each addition with a hand mixer or stand mixer until combined. Beat 1 minute after all eggs are added to form a thick, sticky batter.
6. Transfer batter to a large zip-top bag, squeeze out air, and seal. Snip off one corner to make a 1" hole.

(continued ▶)

Cooking Tips

Instead of piping the filling into your éclairs, you can split them lengthwise and spread the filling inside.

7. Pipe batter onto prepared baking sheet in 6"-long lines about 1" apart from one another. Use a wet finger to smooth any points.

8. Bake 15 minutes, then reduce temperature to 350°F and bake another 20 minutes or until golden brown. Don't open oven door while baking.

9. Poke pastries halfway through at each end (this is where you will be filling them) with a skewer or chopstick, then return to oven for about 10 minutes more, until pastries sound hollow when tapped. Let cool completely, about 30 minutes.

10. Beat ½ cup heavy cream in a medium bowl until stiff peaks form, about 5 minutes. Fold into vanilla pudding. Add filling to a large pastry bag or zip-top bag fitted with a large round or star tip. Poke into each side of one pastry and squeeze to fill. Repeat to fill remaining éclairs.

11. Add chocolate chips and remaining ½ cup heavy cream to a medium microwave-safe bowl and microwave for 30-second increments, stirring between each, until smooth. Alternatively, melt over a double boiler.

12. Dip tops of éclairs in chocolate mixture. Serve.

CLOVE AND TOM COLLINS PIE

 "$pringfield (Or, How I Learned to Stop Worrying and Love Legalized Gambling)," Season 5

Cloves, Tom Collins mix, and a frozen pie crust do not a meal make. Even Homer wouldn't eat it. But he'd happily eat this citrusy and creamy pie spiked with gin.

SERVES 8

1 frozen pie crust (in disposable pie pan)

1 (14-ounce) can sweetened condensed milk

4 large egg yolks

½ cup fresh lemon juice

1 heaping tablespoon finely grated lemon zest

1 cup cold heavy whipping cream

2 tablespoons powdered sugar

1–2 tablespoons gin (to taste) or 1 teaspoon vanilla extract

½ teaspoon ground cloves, for garnish

2 lemon slices, for garnish

1. Preheat oven according to instructions on frozen pie crust for baking an empty crust.
2. Following instructions, bake crust until golden brown. Let cool and adjust oven temperature to 350°F.
3. In a medium mixing bowl, combine sweetened condensed milk, egg yolks, lemon juice, and lemon zest. Whisk together and add to baked crust, spreading to make an even layer.
4. Bake about 10 minutes until set. Filling should jiggle slightly in center but not be liquid. Let pie cool completely, then chill until topping is ready.
5. Once pie is cool and chilling, add heavy cream to a separate medium mixing bowl and beat, adding sugar 1 teaspoon at a time while beating. Beat until soft peaks form, then add gin 1 tablespoon at a time (or add vanilla). Continue beating until stiff peaks form, about 5 minutes.
6. Top pie with whipped cream, smoothing to cover. Sprinkle with ground cloves and decorate with lemon slices. Chill until ready to serve, up to a day. Go see Mom.

WHALE OF A WIFE CAKE

 "A Milhouse Divided," Season 8

Celebrate your marriage courtesy of the state gaming commission with a whale-shaped ice cream cake.

SERVES 12

½ gallon chocolate ice cream, slightly softened

½ cup chocolate sauce, at room temperature

8 ounces crisp chocolate cookies, crumbled

½ gallon vanilla ice cream, fully frozen

1 (8-ounce) container whipped topping

Blue food coloring

Optional: 1 round blue candy

1. Cut clean cardboard into one 10" × 14" rectangle for a base and three 14" × 5" strips for sides. Lay strips horizontally and use a box cutter or utility knife to lightly score at every inch (this will allow you to shape the sides of the whale mold).

2. Draw an outline of a whale about 1' long on the base. Using hot glue or packing tape, stand scored cardboard strips upright along the edges of the whale outline and shape them to make a mold. Trim the strips as needed and seal edges where the strips meet with glue or tape.

3. Line whale mold with plastic wrap, covering the entire bottom and all sides. Press into all corners and secure edges of plastic wrap with tape on the outside of the cardboard.

4. Add enough chocolate ice cream to the lined mold to make a 2" layer, spreading evenly and pressing into all corners and edges. Chill in the freezer 2 hours.

5. Remove mold from freezer and top chocolate ice cream with chocolate sauce in an even layer. Top with cookie crumbs. Freeze another 2 hours.

6. Let vanilla ice cream warm up on the counter 30 minutes. Add a 2" layer of vanilla ice cream on top of the cookie crumbs, spreading out evenly and pressing into all corners and edges. Freeze 3 hours.

(continued ▶)

Cooking Tips

You can also make this ice cream cake in a 7" × 11" or 9" × 13" rectangular pan. Allow plenty of time for freezing each layer. You can leave the cake to freeze for longer at any point and come back to it.

7. Meanwhile, fit a small pastry bag or zip-top bag with a small round tip, or cut a ⅛" hole in the corner of the bag, and transfer a heaping ½ cup whipped topping to the bag. In a medium mixing bowl, mix remaining whipped topping with a few drops blue food coloring to tint it baby blue. Place bag and bowl in refrigerator.

8. Once cake is frozen solid, break apart mold and carefully use plastic wrap to move cake to a large platter, then remove plastic wrap. Cover cake in blue whipped topping, smoothing on all sides.

9. Use white whipped topping to spell out "To a Whale of a Wife" on top. Change out the round tip for a star tip, or widen the hole in the bag tip, and use it to decorate the edges in a shell pattern or a similar pattern. Draw a smile and an eye, using blue candy (if using) to make an iris.

10. Freeze cake at least 4 hours or overnight before serving at a first-class wedding reception.

BART'S CHOCOLATE MARSHMALLOWS

 "Marge Be Not Proud," Season 7

If you're old enough to shoplift, then you're old enough to make your own marshmallows. And while these hot cocoa–flavored treats are no substitute for a mother's love, they are incredibly delicious.

MAKES 16–24 MARSHMALLOWS

1 cup cool water, divided

3 (¼-ounce) packets unflavored powdered gelatin

1½ cups granulated sugar

1 cup light corn syrup

⅛ teaspoon salt

½ cup plus 2 tablespoons cocoa powder, sifted, divided

2 teaspoons vanilla extract

2 tablespoons powdered sugar

1. Line an 8" or 9" square pan with parchment paper and grease paper and pan with nonstick cooking spray. Grease a rubber spatula.
2. Add ½ cup water and gelatin to a large mixing bowl or the bowl of a stand mixer fitted with the whisk attachment and combine. Set aside.
3. Combine remaining ½ cup water, sugar, corn syrup, and salt in a deep heavy saucepan. Stir over medium heat until sugar dissolves. Stop stirring and turn up heat to medium-high. Cook until mixture reaches 240°F on a candy thermometer. Remove from heat.
4. Add ½ cup cocoa powder to gelatin mixture and stir with a spatula or whisk. Start mixer on low. Slowly pour hot sugar mixture into gelatin mixture with the mixer running.
5. Once all sugar mixture has been added, turn mixer up to high and beat 10 minutes or until mixture is shiny and fluffy and holds soft peaks (if using a hand mixer, this may take longer than 10 minutes). Just before you're done mixing, add vanilla.

(continued ▶)

Cooking Tips

While you can use a hand mixer, a stand mixer is highly recommended. Store for up to 1 week in an airtight container with parchment paper or wax paper separating the layers.

6. Add mixture to prepared pan and, if needed, spread level with the greased spatula.
7. Combine remaining 2 tablespoons cocoa powder and powdered sugar in a small bowl. Sift about $1/3$ powdered sugar mixture onto top of marshmallow mixture. Reserve the rest for later. Let marshmallow mixture sit on the counter, uncovered, for at least 6 hours or overnight.
8. Sift remaining powdered sugar mixture onto a clean surface. Turn out marshmallow onto the prepared surface and peel away parchment paper.
9. Oil a circle cookie cutter or sharp chef's knife and cut marshmallows into circles or squares. Coat all sides of marshmallows in sifted powdered sugar mix to prevent sticking. Eat with a fork and knife.

A BIG PILE OF BROWNIES

 "Homer's Barbershop Quartet," Season 5

Oh my god! Oh my god! It's A Big Pile of Brownies! If you're hosting a party, you'll need plenty of dessert. These moist and rich chocolate brownies are sure to disappear fast.

**MAKES ABOUT
30 BROWNIES**

1½ cups (3 sticks) unsalted butter
2½ cups granulated sugar
6 large eggs, beaten
1¾ cups Dutch-process cocoa
   powder
1 tablespoon vanilla extract
2 cups all-purpose flour
1½ teaspoons espresso powder
1½ teaspoons baking powder
1½ teaspoons salt
3 cups semisweet chocolate chips

1. Preheat oven to 350°F and lightly grease a rimmed half sheet pan with nonstick cooking spray (roughly 12" × 18" × 1").
2. Add butter and sugar to a medium microwave-safe bowl. Microwave in 30-second increments, stirring between each, until butter is melted and sugar is beginning to melt. Alternatively, cook over medium-low heat in a saucepan, stirring constantly.
3. In a large mixing bowl, stir together eggs, cocoa powder, and vanilla. Add warm butter mixture slowly while stirring. Mix until incorporated.
4. Sift flour, espresso powder, baking powder, and salt on top of wet mixture. Add chocolate chips. Fold flour and chocolate chips into batter until just combined.
5. Add batter to prepared pan and spread to even. Bake in center of oven 20–28 minutes until a toothpick inserted in the middle comes out with just a few crumbs attached.
6. Let brownies cool in the pan, about 1 hour. Refrigerate for at least 1 hour before cutting for perfectly square brownies.

Cooking Tips

If you're not serving a big crowd (or one Homer), you can cut the ingredients by half and bake in a greased 9" × 9" or 8" × 11" pan for 28–35 minutes.

FLOOR PIE

 "Boy Scoutz 'n the Hood," Season 5

Practice your trap-setting skills and pie-making skills in one fell swoop. This classic cherry pie is sure to earn you a badge and nab a hungry Homer too.

SERVES 8

3 (15-ounce) cans pitted sour cherries in water or light syrup, 2 drained, 1 undrained

1 cup granulated sugar, plus 2 teaspoons for topping

¼ cup quick-cooking tapioca

1½ teaspoons vanilla extract

½ teaspoon salt

⅛ teaspoon nutmeg

Optional: Red food coloring

2 prepared pie crusts (not in disposable pan), divided

1 large egg

1 tablespoon water

1. Combine cherries and liquid, 1 cup sugar, tapioca, vanilla, salt, nutmeg, and red food coloring (if using) in a large mixing bowl. Set aside.
2. Arrange an oven rack near the bottom of the oven. Preheat oven to 425°F. Line a large rimmed baking sheet with aluminum foil.
3. Line a 9" pie pan with 1 pie crust. Pour in cherry filling. Beat egg with water in a small bowl and paint edges of dough.
4. Cover with second pie crust. Press crusts together and crimp edges along pan.
5. Paint top of crust with more egg wash and sprinkle with remaining 2 teaspoons sugar. Cut a few steam vents into top of pie.
6. Place pie on prepared baking sheet and bake on bottom rack about 45 minutes or until filling is bubbly and crust is browned.
7. Let cool completely (at least 3 hours) before cutting and serving.

Cooking Tips

Decrease sugar to ³/₄ cup if using cherries in light syrup. You can use frozen sour cherries instead: Defrost 5 heaping cups cherries in a bowl. Use cherries and ³/₄ cup of the liquid in place of the canned cherries in this recipe.

BLOODY SPEARHEAD COOKIES

 "Miracle on Evergreen Terrace," Season 9

It just takes a little icing to transform spiced Christmas tree cookies into something much cooler: Bloody Spearhead Cookies. You can decorate some cookies with green icing to make festive trees for a more traditional treat.

MAKES ABOUT 40 COOKIES

2½ cups all-purpose flour, plus more for dusting

1½ teaspoons baking powder

¾ teaspoon salt

1½ teaspoons ground cinnamon

1 teaspoon ground ginger

¼ teaspoon ground cloves

¼ teaspoon ground nutmeg

1 cup (2 sticks) unsalted butter, at room temperature

1 cup packed dark brown sugar

¼ cup granulated sugar

1 large egg

2 tablespoons molasses

1 (4¼-ounce) tube black icing

1 (1-ounce) tube red icing

1. Whisk together flour, baking powder, salt, cinnamon, ginger, cloves, and nutmeg in a medium mixing bowl. Set aside.
2. Add butter, brown sugar, and granulated sugar to a large mixing bowl. Beat 3 minutes until light and fluffy. Add egg and molasses and beat another 1–2 minutes, until creamy.
3. Add ½ of the dry mixture to the wet mixture and beat until most dry ingredients are incorporated. Add remaining dry mixture and beat until just combined. Cover dough and chill 1 hour in the refrigerator.
4. Preheat oven to 350°F and line a large baking sheet with parchment paper.
5. Dust a clean work surface with flour. Remove ½ of the dough from refrigerator and quickly form it into a ball. Roll dough out into a circle about ¼" thick, dusting the top lightly with flour as needed.

(continued ▶)

Cooking Tips

This dough freezes well for up to 3 months. it thaw in the refrigerator before using.

6. Use a cookie cutter to cut out tree shapes, working quickly so dough doesn't become too warm. Place cookies on the prepared baking sheet about 1" apart. Place scraps back in the refrigerator with remaining dough.

7. Bake 12 minutes or until lightly browned around the edges and underneath. Lift parchment paper with cookies on top and carefully place it on a cooling rack to cool completely, about 30 minutes.

8. Roll out remaining dough and cut into tree shapes, placing scraps back in the refrigerator. Repeat baking and rerolling to make about 40 cookies.

9. Once all cookies are cool, decorate them to look like bloody spears using red and black icing. Pretend to stab yourself.

HOT FUDGE SUNDAES WITH TEQUILA ICE CREAM

 "Homer Alone," Season 3

Pretend you're at Rancho Relaxo and make this creamy margarita ice cream topped with decadent hot fudge. For a kid-friendly, quicker version, use store-bought vanilla ice cream and skip the tequila in the Hot Fudge.

SERVES 6

For Ice Cream

¾ cup granulated sugar
Zest of 2 small limes
2⅓ cups heavy whipping cream
⅔ cup whole milk
½ teaspoon salt
¼ cup fresh lime juice
3 tablespoons tequila

1. Freeze an ice cream maker bowl as recommended by manufacturer's instructions (usually 6 or more hours).
2. To make Ice Cream: Add sugar and lime zest to a small bowl and rub together using your fingers until well combined.
3. Add heavy cream, milk, salt, and sugar mixture to a medium saucepan over medium heat. Cook, stirring, until mixture comes to a simmer and the sugar has dissolved, about 5 minutes. Remove from heat and let cool to room temperature, about 30 minutes.
4. Add lime juice and tequila and stir. Chill in refrigerator until very cold, at least 3 hours up to 24 hours.
5. Add mixture to ice cream maker and churn according to machine's instructions until mixture thickens greatly and resembles thick soft serve. Ice Cream can be used immediately for sundaes or stored in an airtight container in freezer up to 1 week.

(continued ▶)

Cooking Tips

Reposado tequila brings the best flavor to the ice cream and hot fudge. For a shortcut, use store-bought hot fudge.

For Hot Fudge and Sundae

⅔ cup heavy whipping cream
½ cup light corn syrup
¼ cup granulated sugar
¼ cup cocoa powder
3 tablespoons unsalted butter
¼ teaspoon salt
1 cup semisweet chocolate chips
Optional: 1–2 tablespoons tequila, to taste
Toppings: Whipped cream, 6 maraschino cherries

6. To make Hot Fudge: Combine heavy cream, corn syrup, sugar, cocoa powder, butter, and salt in a small saucepan. Stir over medium heat until melted, then simmer about 3 minutes.

7. Remove from heat and add chocolate chips. Stir until melted, then add tequila (if using) and stir. Let cool about 3 minutes to thicken up before using, or cover and store in the refrigerator up to 1 month and reheat as needed.

8. When ready to serve, add 2–3 scoops Ice Cream to each of six medium bowls. Top with Hot Fudge followed by whipped cream and a cherry. Enjoy while taking a bubble bath.

MR. BURNS'S FIG CAKE

 "Scenes from the Class Struggle in Springfield," Season 7

Welcome a newcomer to your hotbed of exclusionist snobs by spending your afternoon baking a fig cake. While Mr. Burns pickles his figs, these are soaked in booze for a more pleasant experience. Eeeeexcellent.

SERVES 12

For Cake

1 cup chopped dried black figs
¼ cup brandy, spiced rum, or water
½ cup (1 stick) unsalted butter, at room temperature
¾ cup packed light brown sugar
1 teaspoon finely grated orange zest
1 teaspoon baking powder
½ teaspoon salt
½ teaspoon ground cinnamon
¼ teaspoon ground cloves
2 large eggs, at room temperature
1½ cups all-purpose flour
½ cup whole milk
¾ cup chopped toasted walnuts
¼ cup pulp-free orange juice

1. To make Cake: Combine figs and brandy in a small microwave-safe bowl. Microwave about 1 minute until steaming hot, then toss. Alternatively, heat in a small saucepan over medium heat 3 minutes. Let sit 30 minutes, tossing occasionally.

2. Preheat oven to 325°F. Line an 8" or 9" square cake pan with parchment paper, leaving enough overhang to lift out cake once baked.

3. Add butter, brown sugar, orange zest, baking powder, salt, cinnamon, and cloves to a large mixing bowl. Beat about 3 minutes until creamy.

4. Add eggs and beat until well mixed. Add ½ of the flour and mix. Add milk and mix, then add remaining flour and mix until just combined. Fold in soaked figs and walnuts.

5. Add batter to prepared pan and spread evenly. Bake about 30 minutes until a toothpick inserted in the middle comes out clean.

6. Drizzle orange juice over top of cake. Let cake cool completely, about 1 hour, before using parchment paper to lift cake out of pan and onto a platter.

(continued ▶)

Recipe Variations

Swap the figs for your favorite dried fruit. Swap the walnuts for pecans. Replace up to a tablespoon of juice in the Icing for brandy or spiced rum.

For Icing

2 cups plus 1 tablespoon powdered sugar, divided

2½ tablespoons pulp-free orange juice

¼ teaspoon almond extract

Pink and purple food coloring

7. To make Icing: Add 2 cups powdered sugar, 2½ tablespoons orange juice, and almond extract to a small bowl. Mix until creamy, adding more juice if too thick and more powdered sugar if too thin (it should be thin enough to be poured but still completely opaque).

8. Remove 2 heaping tablespoons Icing to a second small bowl. Color larger amount of Icing pink and pour over top of cake, gently spreading to the edges.

9. Add up to 1 more tablespoon powdered sugar to reserved white Icing to make thicker for writing. Color Icing purple and add to an icing bag or plastic bag with a tip cut out. Write "WELCOME HOMER" in creepy letters.

CARAMEL CODS

 "Treehouse of Horror VIII," Season 9

Yar, gather 'round and hear the story of the very first Halloween...I mean, Caramel Cod. Instead of feasting on little children, make fish-shaped cookies dipped in caramel your annual tradition.

**MAKES ABOUT
40 COOKIES**

2½ cups all-purpose flour, plus extra for dusting

1 teaspoon baking powder

½ teaspoon salt

1 cup (2 sticks) unsalted butter, at room temperature

¾ cup plus 1 tablespoon granulated sugar

1 large egg

1½ teaspoons vanilla extract

Red food coloring

Caramel sauce, for dipping

1. Sift flour, baking powder, and salt into a medium mixing bowl. Set aside.

2. Add butter and sugar to a large mixing bowl or the bowl of a stand mixer. Beat with an electric mixer or stand mixer 3 minutes or until fluffy and pale. Scrape down sides. Add egg, vanilla, and food coloring and mix well. You'll want a bright red butter mixture.

3. Add dry ingredients and mix until just completely combined. Divide dough in two, form into 1"-thick rounds, and wrap each in plastic wrap. Chill in refrigerator 1 hour.

4. Preheat oven to 350°F and line two large baking sheets with parchment paper or silicone mats.

5. Lightly dust a clean work surface with flour. Place one dough round on top and dust with flour. Roll dough out, rotating after the first few passes and turning over once before continuing to roll out to ⅛" thickness. Use a little more flour if needed.

Cooking Tips

The Caramel Sauce from Homer's Patented Space-Age Out-of-This-World Moon Waffles (see recipe in Chapter 1) works perfectly for dipping.

Recipe Variations

If you like your fish on a stick, use candy sticks that are oven safe. After cutting out your unbaked cookies, place a stick on top $\frac{1}{3}$ of the way up from the bottom of the cookie. Use a small scrap of dough and cover the stick, carefully blending it with the cookie dough below to encase it. Use a spatula to flip cookie over and place it on the baking sheet, then bake.

6. Use a fish cookie cutter or trace a cutout of a fish with a sharp knife to cut cookies. Transfer cookies to a prepared baking sheet, spacing 1" apart. Bake cookies about 9–12 minutes until lightly browned on bottom. Transfer to a cooling rack.
7. Repeat with remaining dough. Combine any scraps into a round, wrap, and chill, then continue cutting and baking.
8. Let cookies cool, about 30 minutes, then serve with caramel sauce on the side for dipping.

CHAPTER 6
DRINKS

If you're feeling thirsty but you're all out of Duff, use the recipes in this chapter to mix up a few drinks like they taught you at bartending school. Treat yourself to a homemade Squishee, a Krusty Partially Gelatinated Nondairy Gum-Based Beverage, or a refreshing glass of fresh-squozened

Lemon Tree Lemonade. Homer's Homemade Prozac is a nice pick-me-up if you and your party guests are feeling down, and the purple hue and booziness of a Flaming Moe are sure to light your fire. To alcohol! The cause of, and solution to, all of life's problems.

FLAMING MOE

 "Flaming Moe's," Season 3

Also known as a Flaming Homer, the original drink recipe includes plenty of random alcohol, crème de menthe, and grape cough syrup. These two tasty, medicine-free versions are pleasantly purple, will produce a small flame, and won't make you go blind. The first recipe is a riff on the cosmopolitan; add an extra $1/2$ ounce cranberry juice for a fruitier drink. The second recipe embraces the grape flavor without using Krusty's Non-Narkotik Kough Syrup (for Kids). When made with tequila, it's a unique take on the margarita.

SERVES 1

For Flaming Moe #1

2 ounces vodka
1 ounce cranberry juice cocktail
$1/2$ ounce fresh lime juice
1 teaspoon blue curaçao
Optional: $1/2$ ounce high-proof rum
1 small sprig fresh mint, for garnish

1. Add vodka, cranberry juice, and lime juice to a cocktail shaker or lidded jar filled with ice. Shake until very cold.
2. Strain into a chilled cocktail glass. Add blue curaçao and stir, adding more if desired for color.
3. Slowly and carefully pour rum (if using) into the glass over the back of a spoon. Immediately light with a utility lighter. Don't catch on fire like Lenny— place a heatproof plate over the glass and let the fire go out before consuming. Garnish with mint sprig.

(continued ▶)

Cooking Tips

Different brands of blue curaçao can vary greatly in color
intensity. Start with 1 teaspoon, and if needed, add
a little more until a purple hue is reached.
It can be tricky to light up a cocktail at home.
Use caution and consider enjoying a Flaming Moe
without the fire.

SERVES 1

For Flaming Moe #2

2 ounces blanco tequila or silver rum
1 ounce Concord grape juice
½ ounce fresh lime juice
¼ ounce triple sec
Optional: 1 teaspoon blue curaçao or
    1 small drop blue food coloring,
    for color
Optional: ½ ounce high-proof rum
1 small sprig fresh mint, for garnish

1. Add tequila, grape juice, lime juice, and triple sec to a cocktail shaker or lidded jar filled with ice. Shake until very cold.
2. Strain into a chilled cocktail glass. If desired, add just enough blue curaçao or food coloring to make the mixture purple, then stir.
3. Slowly and carefully pour rum (if using) into the glass over the back of a spoon. Immediately light with a utility lighter. Place a heatproof plate over the glass and let the fire go out before consuming. Garnish with mint sprig.

ADVISORY BOARD FRUIT PUNCH

 "Homer Loves Flanders," Season 5

Serve this drink from the Fruit Punch Advisory Board at your next picnic. They wouldn't give you bad advice, now, would they?

SERVES 4

2 cups cranberry juice cocktail
1 cup freshly squeezed orange juice
¾ cup pineapple juice
2 tablespoons fresh lime juice
1 (12-ounce) can ginger ale or
   sparkling water

1. Add cranberry juice, orange juice, pineapple juice, and lime juice to a large pitcher and stir. Chill in the refrigerator until ready to serve.
2. Top with ginger ale and gently stir. Serve over ice. Let the kids fight it out over Pixy Stix.

Cooking Tips

It's easy to double, triple, or even quadruple this recipe for a crowd.

Recipe Variations

Make it more tropical by swapping the orange juice for mango juice. For a less sweet concoction, use 1½ cups 100% cranberry juice mixed with ½ cup water in place of the cranberry juice cocktail. Leave out the ginger ale or sparkling water altogether for a non-bubbly option. Swap the orange juice or pineapple juice for filtered apple juice. You can also doctor up store-bought bright red fruit punch. Mix up according to the package directions and add pineapple juice and orange juice to taste. Stir and, if desired, top with soda.

SQUISHEES

 "Boy Scoutz 'n the Hood," Season 5

When you're craving an ice-cold sugar injection, it's usually time to visit your local Kwik-E-Mart. But with this homemade Squishees recipe, you can have your choice of flavors and go on a sweet bender anytime.

SERVES 4

For Ice Cream Maker Recipe

4 cups cold water
1 cup granulated sugar
1 (0.16-ounce) packet powdered drink mix

1. Freeze an ice cream maker bowl according to manufacturer's instructions (usually 6 or more hours).
2. Add cold water, sugar, and drink mix to a large bowl and mix until sugar and powder have dissolved.
3. Add mixture to ice cream maker and churn about 20 minutes or until desired consistency is achieved.
4. Serve immediately in chilled glasses with straws.

SERVES 4

For Blender Recipe

2 cups cold water
1 cup granulated sugar
1 (0.16-ounce) packet powdered drink mix
4 cups ice cubes

1. Combine cold water, sugar, and drink mix in a blender. Add ice and blend until smooth.
2. Serve immediately in chilled glasses with straws.

Recipe Variations

For a less sweet Squishee, use 3/4 cup sugar.
To make a Super Squishee:
Only make this flavor-packed version if you're ready for an intense sugar high and a crushing hangover. Reduce the water by half to make 2 insanely sweet drinks or double the sugar and drink mix to make 4.

SIMPSON & SON REVITALIZING TONIC

 "Grampa vs. Sexual Inadequacy," Season 6

Step right up, folks, and get your Simpson & Son Revitalizing Tonic! Put some ardor in your larder with a mixture of caffeinated ingredients that energize and aphrodisiacs that tantalize. The results of this sweet, spicy, and refreshing tonic are not guaranteed, but it will put some pep in your step!

SERVES 4

½ heaping cup medium-ground coffee
1 tablespoon cocoa powder
1 cinnamon stick, smashed
¼ teaspoon peppercorns, smashed
3 cups boiling water
2 heaping tablespoons honey
3 cups cold soda water

1. Place coffee, cocoa powder, cinnamon, and peppercorns in a heatproof container. Pour boiling water over coffee and spices and stir. Let brew 5 minutes.
2. Stir and strain through a coffee filter. Add honey and stir until dissolved. Refrigerate until cold, at least 1 hour.
3. When ready to serve, fill four glasses or bottles halfway with chilled coffee mixture and top off with soda water. Gently stir. Give your kids fifty bucks and send them to the movies.

Cooking Tips

The coffee mixture can be stored in the refrigerator for up to 3 days. Give it a stir or shake and top with soda water just before serving. Add more honey if you like your coffee drinks extra sweet. The 1:1 mixture of coffee to soda is a nice balance, but feel free to adjust the ratio to suit your tastes.

CORN NOG

Corn Nog might be one of the only things left at the Kwik-E-Mart during a hurricane, but unlike Wadded Beef and Creamed Eels, it's actually delicious. A take on the Central American and Mexican drink *atole*, this egg-free sweet corn beverage will warm you up during inclement weather.

SERVES 6

4 ears fresh sweet corn, shucked
1/2 cup water
4 cups whole milk
1/3–1/2 cup granulated sugar, to taste
1 cinnamon stick
1/8 teaspoon salt
Optional: 1/2 teaspoon vanilla extract
Ground cinnamon, for garnish

1. Working over a large bowl, cut corn from cobs and scrape juice from cobs using the back of a knife. Reserve 2 cobs.
2. Add corn and juice to a blender with water. Blend until very smooth.
3. Add corn mixture to a large saucepan along with milk, sugar, cinnamon, and salt and stir. Start with 1/3 cup sugar, taste, and add more as desired. Add 2 reserved corncobs.
4. Bring to a boil over medium heat while stirring gently. Once boiling, reduce to a low simmer and cook 20 minutes, stirring often to keep milk from scorching.
5. Discard corncobs and add vanilla (if using) and stir. For a thicker drink, serve as is. For a smoother drink, strain through a fine-mesh strainer, pressing mixture with a rubber spatula or wooden spoon.
6. Serve warm in six drinking glasses topped with a dusting of cinnamon.

Recipe Variations

You can substitute part or all of the sugar for honey, if desired. As with eggnog, you can add a little booze to make this drink extra festive. Add about 1/2 ounce dark rum to a 6-ounce serving.

HOMER'S HOMEMADE PROZAC

 "Homer Badman," Season 6

If you're feeling down, try self-medicating with a big bowl of Homer's Homemade Prozac. It may not contain any of the drug's active ingredients, but it does make a great nonalcoholic party punch.

SERVES 20

- 1 (2-liter) bottle ginger ale
- 1 (32-ounce) bottle 100% dark sweet cherry juice
- ½ gallon vanilla ice cream, slightly softened

Add ginger ale and cherry juice to a large punch bowl. Gently stir. Stir in scoops of vanilla ice cream until desired taste is reached. Serve to depressed guests.

Cooking Tips

If you're serving a small crowd, use the ratio of 1 small scoop of ice cream per person with a ratio of 2:1 soda to juice.

Recipe Variations

Swap the ginger ale for ginger beer or a lemon-lime soda like Sprite or 7UP, or use a flavored seltzer for a lighter, less sugary punch. For a classy adult punch, use 1½ bottles sparkling wine and 1 liter ginger ale. Swap the cherry juice for cranberry or cran-raspberry juice cocktail. Or, for a sweeter rendition, use Hawaiian Punch. Swap the vanilla ice cream for a fruit sherbet like orange, berry, or pineapple. Use a nondairy vanilla ice cream to make it vegan.

Lemonade
25¢

LEMON TREE LEMONADE

 "Lemon of Troy," Season 6

You could make lemonade like Bart and Milhouse make it: a squeeze of lemon topped off with a huge mound of sugar. But unless you want to chew your drink, add some water for a refreshing summertime beverage that's a million times better than turnip juice.

SERVES 6

1 cup fresh-squozened lemon juice
1 cup granulated sugar
6 cups cold water

Add lemon juice and sugar to a medium pitcher or large liquid measuring cup. Mix until sugar is dissolved. Add water and mix. Chill in the refrigerator until ready to serve (up to 3 days).

Cooking Tips

This recipe can be sized up or down easily. Just keep the proportions 1 part juice, 1 part sugar, and 6 parts water.

Recipe Variations

For a tarter, less sweet lemonade, add less sugar to taste. For sparkling lemonade, swap half of the water for sparkling water. Add just before serving. For limeade, swap all or part of the lemon juice for lime juice. For an Arnold Palmer, mix 1 part lemonade with 1 part unsweetened iced tea. For a Squishee-like frozen lemonade, add 1 part juice, 1 part sugar, 2 parts cold water, and 6 parts ice to a blender and blend until frosty.

WHITE WINE SPRITZER

 "Viva Ned Flanders," Season 10

You only live once, so why not enjoy a few White Wine Spritzers? This recipe doesn't skimp on the vino, and there are plenty of tasty variations on the classic if you want to really go wild like Ned in Vegas.

MAKES 1 COCKTAIL

3 ounces crisp white wine, chilled
1 ounce club soda, chilled
1 lemon, lime, or orange twist or wheel, for garnish

In a large wine or cocktail glass filled with ice, combine wine and club soda. Garnish with citrus peel or place citrus wheel on glass rim. Make some Vegas-style mistakes.

Recipe Variations

Don't just garnish your spritzer with citrus;
add a squeeze or two to the mix as well for a fruity touch.
Add 1 ounce fresh-squeezed grapefruit juice and garnish with a grapefruit
twist. This variation is especially good when paired with a citrus-forward wine.
Add 2 or 3 dashes of bitters for a slightly aromatic, spiced note.
Fruit-flavored bitters like orange, lemon, or grapefruit work best
with fruity wines, while Angostura bitters are best
when used with dry, more herbal wines.
Add up to 1 ounce Campari or Aperol for an Italian-style spritz.
Swap the club soda for your favorite flavored seltzer. Flavors like lemon,
lime, grapefruit, and orange work especially well.

KRUSTY PARTIALLY GELATINATED NONDAIRY GUM-BASED BEVERAGES

 "22 Short Films about Springfield," Season 7

When placing your order at Krusty Burger, feel free to just call these shakes. This homemade coconut treat is gum-free and not really gelatinated, but it is nondairy and a beverage.

SERVES 4

1 (13½-ounce) can full-fat coconut milk, shaken

1 (13½-ounce) can coconut cream, shaken

½ cup granulated sugar

3 tablespoons agave syrup or light corn syrup

¼ teaspoon salt

1½ teaspoons vanilla extract

1 cup nondairy milk

Optional: Vegan chocolate syrup or strawberry sauce

1. Freeze ice cream maker bowl as recommended by manufacturer's instructions (usually 6 or more hours).
2. Combine coconut milk, coconut cream, sugar, agave, and salt in a medium saucepan. Heat over medium heat and bring to a simmer, stirring constantly. Simmer about 3 minutes until sugar is just dissolved and mixture is smooth.
3. Remove from heat and let cool to room temperature, about 30 minutes. Add vanilla and stir. Chill in refrigerator until very cold, 3 hours or overnight.
4. Add mixture to ice cream maker and churn according to the machine's instructions until mixture resembles thick soft-serve ice cream.
5. To make a shake, add 2 scoops ice cream to a milkshake glass or blender. Add up to ¼ cup nondairy milk (or just enough to get the blender going) and chocolate syrup or strawberry sauce (if using). Process until smooth and creamy. Repeat to make 4 shakes. Ice cream can also be frozen in an airtight container up to 1 week.

Cooking Tips

Make a quicker version using store-bought partially gelatinated nondairy gum-based ice cream.

BART'S "SUPOIB" MANHATTAN

 "Bart the Murderer," Season 3

No one mixes up a Manhattan like Bart, but you can come close by using his recipe. This is a classic drink beloved by mobsters everywhere, so don't mess it up: A flat, flavorless Manhattan will get you the kiss of death.

SERVES 1

1 jigger (1½ ounces) bourbon or rye
½ ounce Italian sweet vermouth
1 dash (about ⅛ teaspoon)
   Angostura bitters
1 maraschino or brandied cherry

In a cocktail shaker or large glass, stir bourbon, vermouth, and bitters with cracked ice until thoroughly chilled. Strain into a cocktail glass and garnish with cherry.

Cooking Tips

Don't skimp on the bourbon or vermouth. There are only a few ingredients in this classic cocktail, so quality matters. A regular bright red maraschino cherry will work, but a dark, flavorful cocktail cherry (like Luxardo) makes a more sophisticated drink.

Recipe Variations

Swap the cherry garnish for an orange peel twist. Swap the bourbon or rye for blended scotch for a Rob Roy. For a less sweet cocktail known as a "perfect" Manhattan, replace half of the sweet vermouth with dry vermouth. Change up the bitters for a slightly different flavor. Peychaud's is similar to Angostura but has a more anise-forward flavor. Orange bitters make the cocktail more aromatic and citrusy, while chocolate bitters play up the vanilla in bourbon.

FLANDERS'S PLANTER'S PUNCH

 "The War of the Simpsons," Season 2

Ned Flanders made some mean mixed drinks before he became a teetotaler. His take on planter's punch is decidedly boozy with plenty of rum and bourbon. Drink responsibly or risk ending up committing some serious party fouls.

**SERVES 2
(OR 1 DRUNK HOMER)**

3 shots (4½ ounces) dark rum
1 jigger (1½ ounces) bourbon
1 little dab-a-roo (1–1½ ounces) crème de cassis, to taste
Optional but Recommended:
  1 ounce fresh lemon juice

Add rum, bourbon, crème de cassis, and lemon juice (if using) to a cocktail shaker or jar filled with ice. Start with 1 ounce crème de cassis and add more to taste as desired. Shake until very cold and strain into a glass filled with ice. Get embarrassingly drunk and wear a lampshade on your head.

Recipe Variations

This makes a high-proof punch. For a little less bite, leave out the bourbon. If you can't get your hands on crème de cassis, try substituting ½–1 ounce grenadine. For a more traditional and tropical take on planter's punch, mix up 4 ounces dark rum, 6 ounces pineapple juice, ½ ounce lime juice, and ½ ounce grenadine. Shake well with ice. Makes 2 generous drinks.

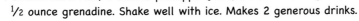

US/METRIC CONVERSION CHART

VOLUME CONVERSIONS

US Volume Measure	Metric Equivalent
⅛ teaspoon	0.5 milliliter
¼ teaspoon	1 milliliter
½ teaspoon	2 milliliters
1 teaspoon	5 milliliters
½ tablespoon	7 milliliters
1 tablespoon (3 teaspoons)	15 milliliters
2 tablespoons (1 fluid ounce)	30 milliliters
¼ cup (4 tablespoons)	60 milliliters
⅓ cup	90 milliliters
½ cup (4 fluid ounces)	125 milliliters
⅔ cup	160 milliliters
¾ cup (6 fluid ounces)	180 milliliters
1 cup (16 tablespoons)	250 milliliters
1 pint (2 cups)	500 milliliters
1 quart (4 cups)	1 liter (about)

WEIGHT CONVERSIONS

US Weight Measure	Metric Equivalent
½ ounce	15 grams
1 ounce	30 grams
2 ounces	60 grams
3 ounces	85 grams
¼ pound (4 ounces)	115 grams
½ pound (8 ounces)	225 grams
¾ pound (12 ounces)	340 grams
1 pound (16 ounces)	454 grams

OVEN TEMPERATURE CONVERSIONS

Degrees Fahrenheit	Degrees Celsius
200 degrees F	95 degrees C
250 degrees F	120 degrees C
275 degrees F	135 degrees C
300 degrees F	150 degrees C
325 degrees F	160 degrees C
350 degrees F	180 degrees C
375 degrees F	190 degrees C
400 degrees F	205 degrees C
425 degrees F	220 degrees C
450 degrees F	230 degrees C

BAKING PAN SIZES

American	Metric
8 × 1½ inch round baking pan	20 × 4 cm cake tin
9 × 1½ inch round baking pan	23 × 3.5 cm cake tin
11 × 7 × 1½ inch baking pan	28 × 18 × 4 cm baking tin
13 × 9 × 2 inch baking pan	30 × 20 × 5 cm baking tin
2 quart rectangular baking dish	30 × 20 × 3 cm baking tin
15 × 10 × 2 inch baking pan	30 × 25 × 2 cm baking tin (Swiss roll tin)
9 inch pie plate	22 × 4 or 23 × 4 cm pie plate
7 or 8 inch springform pan	18 or 20 cm springform or loose bottom cake tin
9 × 5 × 3 inch loaf pan	23 × 13 × 7 cm or 2 lb narrow loaf or pâté tin
1½ quart casserole	1.5 liter casserole
2 quart casserole	2 liter casserole

INDEX

ABOUT THE AUTHOR

Laurel Randolph is a cookbook author and lifelong Simpsons fan. She runs the popular blog and *Instagram* account *The Joy of Cooking Milhouse*, where she makes dishes from classic episodes of *The Simpsons*. She is the author of *The Instant Pot® Electric Pressure Cooker Cookbook: Easy Recipes for Fast & Healthy Meals*; *The Instant Pot® No-Pressure Cookbook: 100 Low-Stress, High-Flavor Recipes*; and *Instant Pot® Desserts: Sweet Recipes for Your Electric Pressure Cooker*. Laurel has written and developed recipes for numerous publications, including *Food52*, *EatingWell*, *Paste* magazine, *The Spruce*, *Serious Eats*, *Kitchen Table* magazine, *Table Matters*, *Los Angeles* magazine, and *Insider*.

THE MAGIC OF DISNEY— IN YOUR KITCHEN!

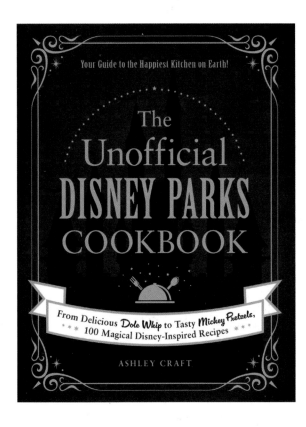

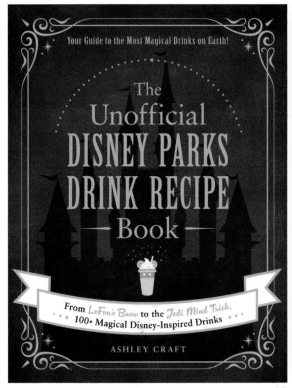

Pick Up or Download Your Copies Today!